# Learning Opportunities for Principals

# Learning Opportunities for Principals

## Methods for Meeting the Needs of Today's Administrators

Edited by
Lee A. Westberry

ROWMAN & LITTLEFIELD
*Lanham • Boulder • New York • London*

Published by Rowman & Littlefield
An imprint of The Rowman & Littlefield Publishing Group, Inc.
4501 Forbes Boulevard, Suite 200, Lanham, Maryland 20706
www.rowman.com

86-90 Paul Street, London EC2A 4NE, United Kingdom

Copyright © 2022 by Lee A. Westberry

*All rights reserved.* No part of this book may be reproduced in any form or by any electronic or mechanical means, including information storage and retrieval systems, without written permission from the publisher, except by a reviewer who may quote passages in a review.

British Library Cataloguing in Publication Information Available

**Library of Congress Cataloging-in-Publication Data Available**

ISBN 9781475865592 (cloth) | ISBN 9781475865608 (pbk.) | ISBN 9781475865615 (epub)

*I would like to dedicate this book to my husband, Danny, who has always supported my work and my dreams. Without which, I would not be where I am today.*

# Contents

Preface     ix
*Dr. Lee A. Westberry*

Acknowledgments     xiii

Introduction     xv

**1**    Building Capacity: Principals Leading Their Own Learning     1
*Sally Zepeda, Salih Cevik, and Sevda Yidririm*

**2**    Communities of Practice: Leading Schools in the Twenty-First Century     17
*R. Stewart Mayers and Jennifer Anderson*

**3**    Principal Mentoring as Professional Learning     31
*Arvin D. Johnson*

**4**    What Is the District's Role in Supporting the Principal?     49
*Sherry Hoyle*

**5**    Principal Evaluation Practices That Support Individual and Organizational Growth     65
*Kevin Badgett and Larry G. Daniel*

**6**    Setting the Destination and Charting the Course: Higher-Education Opportunities for K–12 Leaders Engaged in Systems Improvement     83
*Noelle Paufler*

| | | |
|---|---|---|
| **7** | Building a District Leadership Pipeline<br>*Sherry Hoyle and Aaron Allen* | 97 |

About the Authors　　115

# Preface

## *Principal Support: The Need*

Dr. Lee A. Westberry

School principals face many challenges today that did not exist twenty years ago. The intense focus on instructional supervision (Comighud et al., 2020; McGhee & Stark, 2021; Westberry, 2021), the addition of social media and its impact (Abbas et al., 2019; Ansari & Khan, 2020), the transition from management to leadership (Connolly & Fertig, 2019; Daniels et al., 2019), and school finance and equity issues (Baker, 2021; Dhaliwal & Bruno, 2021) are just a few factors to consider.

Additional factors include teacher shortages (Farley & Chamberlain, 2021; Fredericova, 2021), increased school violence (Bell, 2021; Thornton, 2021), technology and virtual elements of school (Dogan et al., 2021; Kingsbury, 2021), and the more recent COVID-19 pandemic and its impact on schooling (Huck & Zhang, 2021; Westberry et al., 2021). How principals fare in this high demand environment can largely depend on the support provided and the continued professional learning received.

To distinguish between the two factors, one must understand the difference. Principal support can be defined as the assistance or reinforcement provided to a principal to help him/her function at the prescribed levels of expectation. This support can come in many forms, such as communities of practice, mentoring, district support, coaching, principal evaluation, higher-education participation, and leadership pipelines. This book will highlight each of these areas and how they provide support for principals to effectively do their jobs. The need will be highlighted and expounded upon with suggestions on how to implement effective support systems for administrators.

Principal learning, on the other hand, refers to the context of the learning. How do principals stay current in school law issues that impact their schools? How do principals learn how to implement effective systems in order to

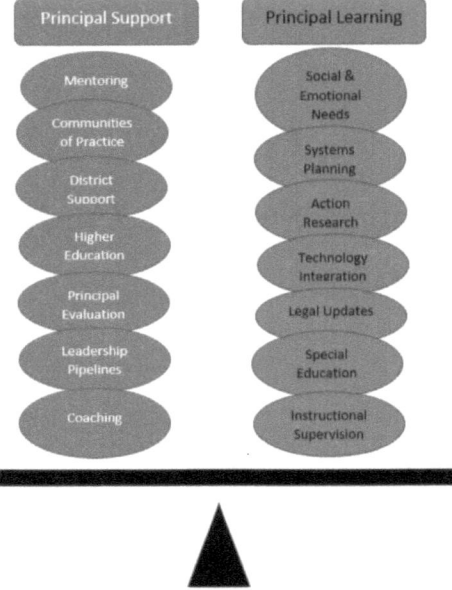

Figure 0.1 Principal Support versus Principal Learning Balance.

operate effectively and efficiently? How do principals learn about special education issues that have an impact on technological innovations? These are just a few questions to consider.

Each of these areas and more can be learned through the support mechanisms described before; therefore, principal support and principal learning are not mutually exclusive. The trick is to combine the two to maximize results, which increases principal self-efficacy, or the belief that one can do his/her job effectively (Bandura, 1977). Consider figure 0.1 when thinking about these two factors: principal support and principal learning.

Each of the support vehicles must be attuned to the learning needed. Sit-and-get meetings do not produce the desired learning (Westberry & Hornor, 2022), as learning takes time and must be practiced. In addition, the support vehicle must be the best fit for the learning required. In essence, districts must consider the skill sets and knowledge of those leading the support efforts, the resources available, and the culture of the district in order to effectively implement principal supports that net principal learning. Without properly evaluating these elements and the preparedness for support and learning, even the best efforts will not produce the desired outcomes.

Understanding that these elements are not all inclusive of principal support systems or the needed principal learning, they do represent the most pertinent needs for today's administrators. Striking a balance between the two (support and learning) is crucial for district planning. Without this planning up front, districts inevitably create an imbalance and therefore are not capitalizing on their most valued assets: their people.

## REFERENCES

Abbas, J., Aman, J., Nurunnabi, M., & Bano, S. (2019). The impact of social media on learning behavior for sustainable education: Evidence of students from selected universities in Pakistan. *Sustainability, 11*(6), 1683.

Ansari, J. A. N., & Khan, N. A. (2020). Exploring the role of social media in collaborative learning the new domain of learning. *Smart Learning Environments, 7*(1), 1–16.

Baker, B. D. (2021). *Educational inequality and school finance: Why money matters for America's students*. Harvard Education Press.

Bandura, A. (1977). Self-efficacy: Toward a unifying theory of behavioral change. *Psychological Review, 84*(2), 191–215.

Bell, C. (2021). *Suspended: Punishment, violence, and the failure of school safety*. JHU Press.

Comighud, S., Futalan, M., & Cordevilla, R. (2020). Instructional supervision and performance evaluation: A correlation of factors [Conference session]. UBT International Conference, Pristine, Kosovo, p. 193.

Connolly, M., James, C., & Fertig, M. (2019).The difference between educational management and educational leadership and the importance of educational responsibility. *Educational Management Administration & Leadership, 47*(4), 504–519.

Daniels, E., Hondeghem, A., & Dochy, F. (2019). A review on leadership and leadership development in educational settings. *Educational Research Review, 27*, 110–125.

Dhaliwal, T. K., & Bruno, P. (2021).The rural/nonrural divide? K–12 district spending and implications of equity-based school funding. *AERA Open, 7*.

Dogan, N. A., Dawson, K., & Ritzhaupt, A. D. (2021). Do school levels matter? How elementary, middle, and high school teachers differ in their perceptions and use of technology. *Journal of Educational Technology Systems, 49*(4), 432–460.

Farley, A. N., & Chamberlain, L. M. (2021). The teachers are not alright: A call for research and policy on teacher stress and well-being. *The New Educator, 7*(3), 305–323.

Federičová, M. (2021). Teacher turnover: What can we learn from Europe? *European Journal of Education, 56*(1), 102–116.

Huck, C., & Zhang, J. (2021). Effects of the COVID-19 pandemic on K-12 education: A systematic literature review. *New Waves-Educational Research and Development Journal, 24*(1), 53–84.

Kingsbury, I. (2021). Online learning: How do brick and mortar schools stack up to virtual schools? *Education and Information Technologies, 26*, 6567–6588.

McGhee, M. W., & Stark, M. D. (2021). Empowering teachers through instructional supervision: Using solution focused strategies in a leadership preparation program. *Journal of Educational Supervision, 4*(1), 43.

Thornton, F. (2021). Teacher trauma in the age of school violence. In Kjersti VanSlyke-Briggs & Elizabeth Bloom (Eds.), *Dress rehearsals for gun violence: Confronting trauma and anxiety in America's schools* (p. 57). Rowman & Littlefield Lanham, MD.

Westberry, L. (2020). *Putting the pieces together: A systems approach to school leadership.* Rowman & Littlefield.

Westberry, L., Hornor, T., & Murray, K. (2021). The need of the virtual principal amid the pandemic. *International Journal of Education Policy and Leadership, 17*(10).

Westberry, L. & Hornor, T. (2022). Best practices in principal professional development. *AASA Journal of Scholarship and Practice, 19*(1), 29–47.

# Acknowledgments

I would like to acknowledge all of the wonderful educational leaders who keep learning and growing for the sake of our children. You are not alone. I would also like to acknowledge all of the contributors to this volume. Their work serves to support educators across the nation. Thank you for your tireless efforts.

# Introduction

*Learning Opportunities for Principals: Methods for Meeting the Needs of Today's Administrators* is a compilation of research from practitioners and professionals across the nation. Each chapter is designed to provide insight into the learning needed for principals and how that can best be achieved. Topics were selected based on principal feedback as to how principals best learn today to stay current and confident.

Knowing that "sit and get" meetings are not the best method of principal learning, each chapter highlights a "how to" approach for principals and district leaders to consider. The insight shared is derived from years of experience in the field as either a participant in the learning or the organizer of that learning. Additionally, each chapter includes a summary and reflection questions for further thought and inquiry.

The authors' biographical information is included for each chapter so that the reader may contact the authors for additional information or support needed. The journey to continue to improve our schools is not a singular or lonely one, as resources are available.

*Chapter 1*

# Building Capacity

## *Principals Leading Their Own Learning*

Sally Zepeda, Salih Cevik, and Sevda Yidririm

### INTRODUCTION

In an effective school, a positive culture provides the foundation for leading and learning. Excellent leaders support the individual and collective growth of their teachers by providing highly personalized learning opportunities embedded not only in the work they do with students in their classrooms but also in the work they do with their colleagues in and out of their classrooms. Principals cannot fully lead learning unless they are actively engaged in gaining knowledge and refining the skills needed to grow their leadership capacity.

Highly successful principals spend the time and exert the effort needed to create the conditions to build relationships while simultaneously improving the instructional program (Honig & Rainey, 2014; Leithwood et al., 2019; Zepeda et al., 2015). Although effective principals build teacher capacity, they need to look inwardly at the types, duration, and context-specific professional development they need to lead their own learning. Principals must become the leaders of learning championing their own growth.

With issues of teacher shortages showing no sign of abatement, trailing second are principal shortages, and the need for qualified principal candidates "will grow 6 percent nationwide by the year 2022" (National Association of Secondary School Principals, 2017, p. 2). This anticipated shortage creates a gap given that during the 2017–2018 school year, public schools employed approximately 90,900 principals and 98,250 assistant principals (US Department of Education, 2020). Exacerbating these gaps, Levin and Bradley (2019) underscore:

The national average tenure of principals in their schools was four years as of 2016–17. This number masks considerable variation, with 35 percent of principals being at their school for less than two years, and only 11 percent of principals being at their school for 10 years or more. (p. 3)

They continue, "overall, approximately 18 percent of principals were no longer in the same position one year later. In high-poverty schools, the turnover rate was 21 percent" (p. 3).

There is urgency for school districts to promote principal learning so that they become the lead learners in their buildings, supporting a culture by modeling what it takes to learn from practice (Lanoue & Zepeda, 2018; Westberry & Horner, 2022; Zepeda et al., 2021). Central office leadership must focus considerable effort on "building the capacity of school principals to lead for instructional improvement within their schools" (Honig et al., 2010, p. v).

Central office leadership support is, however, just one aspect of principal learning. To lead requires principals to learn from the work they enact and through the interactions they have with teachers, students, and others in their own buildings. From this work, leaders can link what they are learning while leading. This type of engagement situates the principal as an active learner. Principals need professional learning embedded in the very work they do with opportunities to engage with others who fulfill similar roles.

It is clear that today and into the foreseeable future, principals must become purposeful about their own professional learning because leading schools has become more complex. The complex nature of the work requires ongoing professional learning opportunities that provide principals "with the understandings, skills, and dispositions needed to respond to the ever-changing school environments and to promote excellence and equity in all schools" (Honig & Rainey, 2014, p. 25).

There are a variety of ways in which principals engage in professional learning to support the development of practices aimed to increase their growth while simultaneously increasing the capacity of their schools. But the question remains, are the current types, duration, and focus of professional learning for principals enough?

This chapter examines, broadly, professional learning that supports principal development. The key attributes of professional learning are examined with a focus on the three cornerstones—reflection, inquiry, and conversations—that embed learning opportunities for principals. Next, the promising practices related to principal professional learning are examined: coaching, virtual and social networks, action research, and conversation walks. A summary and guiding questions conclude the chapter.

## STEPPING INTO THE PRINCIPALSHIP

Principals must be in a position to lead their own learning given the contextual differences of school settings, the culture of the schools in which they lead, and, of course, their own career stages and experiences as leaders. The career path into the principalship is also worth thinking about related to professional learning given that serving as an assistant principal is often the steppingstone to the principalship (Barnett et al., 2017; Goldring et al., 2021; Hitt & Player, 2018).

Other pathways include school district models aimed at growing current assistant principals through context-specific professional development (Gurley et al., 2015) and state department support programs for sitting and aspiring assistant principals (Liang & Augustine-Shaw, 2016).

Under the "old" pathway, assistant principals engaged primarily with issues related to discipline, bus duty, and school facilities (Marshall & Hooley, 2006). With a new view, more pathways for assistant principals allow them to assume more instructional leadership responsibilities (Master et al., 2020) as they are socialized to the position and role of principal (Bengtson et al., 2013).

Unfortunately, too many assistant principals do not engage in professional learning opportunities preparing them for the work of being a principal (Barnett et al., 2017; Gordon, 2020), and as a result, they step into the role not fully prepared to lead the instructional program (Allen & Weaver, 2014; Westberry, 2020). Regardless of pathway, learning to lead is a long-term proposition that requires systems of leader support and professional development across the career continuum.

## LEANING INTO PROFESSIONAL LEARNING FOR PRINCIPALS

Everything we know about job-embedded learning suggests its strength occurs through collaborative practices that are tailored to the needs of the learner and situated in practice. Professional learning should serve as a system of leader support for principals (Westberry, 2020). However, the literature is clear and consistent that much of what leaders (similar to teachers and superintendents) experience from professional learning is episodic, fragmented, and disconnected from the real work and challenges of a principal (Parylo et al., 2013; Zepeda et al., 2017, 2021).

The legacy of ineffective professional development follows the trail of one-day workshops that rarely provide the types of learning to support principals leading their schools. Levin et al. (2020) report findings from the

National Association of Elementary School Principals (NAESP) survey that indicate principals want professional learning that is sustained over time in such areas as building collegial and collaborative work environments and designing professional learning opportunities for teachers and other staff.

## Attributes of Professional Learning

The attributes of high-quality professional development that supports learning are well-documented (Darling-Hammond et al., 2017; Desimone & Garet, 2015; Zepeda, 2019). Professional development is effective when it is content-focused, includes active learning, incorporates coaching support, and provides multiple opportunities for feedback and reflection (Darling-Hammond et al., 2017).

Principals need professional learning that extends over time, includes follow-up, connects to the work of leading, and promotes inquiry and reflection (Parylo & Zepeda, 2015). When these attributes are present, professional learning is job-embedded. Job-embedded professional learning for principals

Table 1.1 Applying Desimone's Core Features to Principal Professional Development

| *Desimone's Core Features for Professional Development* | *Applications to Principal Professional Development* |
| --- | --- |
| Content Focus | • Focus on support for teaching and learning (Hallinger & Murphy, 2012; Zepeda & Lanoue, 2017).<br>• Leading the school and community (Kempa et al., 2017; Kanokorn et al., 2014); management of personnel, finance, and programs (DeMatthews, 2014; Mestry, 2017). |
| Active Learning | • Hands-on learning experiences (Gumus & Bellibas, 2016) that include problem-based learning (Hallinger & Bridges, 2017). |
| Coherence | • Focused professional learning is tied to other support structures such as coaching (Zepeda & Lanoue, 2017). |
| Duration | • Continuous training and development (Rowland, 2017),<br>• Ongoing professional support throughout the careers—especially for early career principals (Rogers & VanGronigen, 2021). |
| Collective Participation | • Networks of administrators (Rowland, 2017)<br>• Learning communities (De Voto & Reedy, 2019; Psencik & Brown, 2018; Westberry & Horner, 2022)<br>• Coaching and mentoring (Pariente & Tubin, 2021). |

would include support from coaches as well as opportunities to engage with peers within and external to their school district.

Desimone (2011a, 2011b) identifies five core features for professional development. Examining these core features and applying them to principal professional development is landscaped in table 1.1.

When these core features and practices are implemented with appropriate support, leaders can thoughtfully improve their practices. The cornerstones—reflection and inquiry and conversations—help to embed learning as a continuous practice for principals.

## EMBEDDING PROFESSIONAL LEARNING CORNERSTONES

Reflection and inquiry and conversations are the cornerstones needed for principal professional learning regardless of the format, the context of the school, or experience and longevity in the position. The cornerstones support learning that is job-embedded and leads more directly to the transfer of knowledge from theory to applications in practice. It is, in part, through inquiry, reflection, and collaborative problem-solving that supports learning from practice.

### Adapted from Desimone (2011a, 2011b)

The objective of all learning should be the translations of theory into practice. To achieve this objective, leaders must engage in making sense of their practices within the context of the schools in which they lead. The cornerstones promote highly collaborative learning.

### Reflection and Inquiry

Effective leaders inquire deeply about their work. When principals inquire about their practices, they ask "tough questions"; they seek data to help inform decisions about their practices. Leaders grow their capacity for change when they reflect on their practices and what they are learning. Reflection can occur at the individual level; however, there is tremendous value and benefit when peers inquire and reflect collaboratively. Reflecting with a colleague enables leaders to ask questions, challenge each other's ideas, and think through ways in which they can improve their practices.

Schön (1987) describes two types of reflection—reflection-in-action and reflection-on-action. *Reflection-in-action* helps to reshape action and practices "in the moment" to be able to make judgments based on what is being learned about practice. *Reflection-on-action* occurs after an action. In a sense, reflection-on-action allows leaders to look back to think through the lessons learned from their practices. Through sustained inquiry about practice, leaders pause to reflect by asking critical questions about their practices and then revising practices based on active inquiry over time (see discussion about action research).

Leaders who reflect gain new perspectives on the dilemmas and contradictions inherent in practices, improve judgment, and increase their capacity to take purposeful action based on the knowledge they discover. Conversations provide unique opportunities that support leaders to reflect on their practices with colleagues.

## Conversations

Conversations come in many forms. To reflect further, principals need opportunities to engage in conversations that support the development of skills, reinforce content from professional learning, and explore their practices in leading schools. Conversations support reflection and inquiry when principals have the opportunity to dig deeper into their leadership practices.

Conversations should lead to growth and development (Zepeda et al., 2019), and Cheliotes and Reilly (2012) amplify that they "stimulate thinking, growth, and change that lead[s] to action" (p. 5). Conversations can occur between the principal and a coach, a fellow school leader, a central office leader, and teachers.

Conversations extend formal professional learning; however, the conversation can be professional learning. There is an adage that the more teachers talk about teaching, the better they get at it. The same adage can be applied to leadership in that the more opportunities principals have to engage in conversations, they focus attention on their practices and their impact.

The cornerstones play a starring role that brings knowledge and ideas presented in traditional forms of professional development such as large-scale workshops and seminars to their applications in practice. As the lead learners, principals must continually apply knowledge and skills gained in learning activities. Without such applications, transfer is unlikely.

## PROMISING PRACTICES

There are many forms of formal and informal professional learning. Examined here are coaching, virtual spaces and social networks, action research, and conversation walks. Each practice is described with cues to the cornerstones that are embedded within them. Unpacking the cornerstones—reflection, inquiry, and conversations—gives the opportunity to examine more deeply how these practices can support transfer from theory to application, making learning more profitable for principal growth and development as the lead learner, championing a culture of learning.

## Coaching

In the United States, almost a half of all principals have received or currently receive leadership coaching (Wise & Cavazos, 2017). Coaching often occurs after formal professional learning as a follow-up to examine transfer of skills and knowledge into practice. However, coaching can be a stand-alone professional learning model (Joyce & Showers, 1982). Coaching occurs concurrently with learning. A coach offers feedback, engages in conversation, and enacts role-play and simulations—all to engage in focused examination of practices.

Coaching is a developmental process that uses a "collaborative, reflective, goal-focused relationship" to achieve professional outcomes (Jones et al., 2016, p. 250). Coaching is replete with conversations to support critical reflective skills about practice in the context of the school. Coaching conversations include "questioning, active listening, and appropriate challenge in a supportive and encouraging climate" (van Nieuwerburgh, 2012, p. 17). Coaching conversations that promote growth are not meant to evaluative or judged.

Coaches provide feedback, model practices, broker resources, and prioritize time on task to support instructional leadership development (Goldring et al., 2018; Turnbull et al., 2015). Coaching involves a commitment of time and energy from the principal and the coach. There is general agreement that coaching is a reciprocal process where both the coach and the principal can learn from up-close examination of practices and the coaching, including conversations.

Coaching for school principals "can build will, skill, knowledge, and capacity because it can go where no other professional development has gone before: into the intellect, behaviors, practices, beliefs, values, and feelings of an educator" (Aguilar, 2013, p. 8). To extend professional learning, a coach would follow the principal into practice. From within school systems, principals are often coached by central office leaders or by fellow principals. For coaching to be successful, its processes and intents should not be conflated with principal evaluation systems. That is, coaching is not an evaluation tool.

Through the advent of digital tools and platforms, coaches can engage with principals in real time offering opportunities for timely and responsive support, engagement in problem-posing, and bringing resolution to make room to move onto the refinement of closely related skills.

## Virtual Spaces and Social Networks

The way individuals learn has changed, and "online spaces shape how, when, and why people learn . . . these spaces are rapidly emerging and evolving, and they include both formal and informal spaces for learning" (Gerber et al., 2017, p. 19). Virtual spaces provide adaptive, flexible opportunities to learn new information and to connect with other professionals. Online learning opens opportunities for collaboration at any time in any place eliminating barriers such as time, travel, and cost.

Both synchronous and asynchronous environments serve a purpose and add value to job-embedded learning opportunities. Synchronous learning environments allow people to work together at the same time ("real-time"). For example, leaders across the state gather to hear a guest speaker present about the state-approved teacher evaluation system. Locally, principals meet to share best practices and materials about developing professional learning plans associated with the new teacher evaluation system.

In asynchronous learning environments, people do not participate with one another at the same time. Interaction occurs when it is convenient using social networks to post comments, responses, ideas (e.g., Facebook, Twitter, etc.), email individually or by list-serv (group), and use discussion boards, for example.

Social networks are more than a collection of people that form into a group. In social networks, knowledge is shared, people are connected to one another, practices are examined, and solutions to complex issues are unpacked. Social networks create the space for collaboration and build expertise through the collective of the network that can support leaders in solving the complex problems they encounter.

Membership in a social network can serve to ease isolation. At the building level, there is only one principal and although leaders build teams, the principalship can be lonely. Other principals in the school district can serve as members of a social network. Conversely, principals across the state, even across the globe can also become members of a social network. More global perspectives can widen the coaching pool where members of a social network can provide emotional support and insights about leading and leadership practices. Through virtual spaces, leaders widen their opportunities to learn from others who fulfill similar positions.

The complexities of leading schools have been exacerbated by disruptions associated with the trail of a pandemic, social unrest, climate changes, etc. With the numerous pivots associated with COVID-19 and its trail to the present day, professional learning for principals is evolving to incorporate more online opportunities.

## Action Research

Action research is a suitable professional learning method (Zepeda, 2015, 2019) that has a strong research and practice base (Coghlan, 2019; Glanz,

2014). Principals start by focusing on a problem of practice as a way to seek solutions (Glanz, 2014). The ultimate goal of action research is to encourage educators to become reflective practitioners that allows them to

- examine real-life practices and experiences in the very place in which these practices and experiences occur,
- use a systematic approach (which may become a cyclical and continuous vehicle for ongoing action research),
- develop deeper meanings about their practices with the assistance of a colleague,
- experiment with their practices based upon extended reflection and analysis of data, and
- implement change. (Zepeda, 2019, p. 171)

Principals can engage in action research individually with teachers, other principals, district administrators, and/or university faculty members (Gordon, 2020).

Action research is a set of collaborative practices typically organized in four stages of cyclical inquiry that encompasses (1) selecting a focus; (2) collecting data; (3) analyzing and interpreting data; and (4) taking action (Glanz, 2014).

Within the cyclical stages of action research, leaders focus on one or two very finite areas to study through practices associated with action research. They collect data about these areas; they analyze data; and then they reflect on their leadership practices. During action research, participants engage in conversations, reflect about possible solutions, and further inquire about practices once interventions related to changes in practice have occurred.

Again, action research is cyclical and iterative. Within the stages of action research, time can be used to pause to engage in reflective conversations, consult with a coach, or work with members of social networks. The practical value of action research is that it is embedded in practice, typically sustained over time, and allows principals the opportunity to focus their own learning about leading, while simultaneously targeting an area that can improve their school communities.

## Conversation Walks

At the building level, the principal is the instructional leader of the school. In this role, principals support teachers as they engage students in learning. One type of support is the classroom observation if they lead to conversations about practice, student engagement, and assessment, for example. When teachers learn from their work, students are the benefactors.

Principals can learn about key aspects of being an instructional leader through the process of conversation walks (Zepeda & Lanoue, 2017). Conversation walks should not be confused with classroom observations associated with teacher evaluation systems. A conversation walk is one where the principal and a trusted colleague engage in such activities as observing classrooms, team meetings, or any other activity where principals exert leadership. As in coaching models, conversation walks would include either a central office leader or another building-level observing in classrooms with the principal and then debriefing about what was observed.

Conversation walks as a form of job-embedded learning and gets the principal out of the main office and into the world of classrooms. By setting aside time in the day to engage in conversation walks, distractions are removed for the principal to connect with the work of leading the instructional program. Learning to engage in discussions about what is observed in classrooms is needed to support teachers and the leadership capacity to be able to carry on these types of conversations. The process of conversation walks associated with classroom observations are elaborated in table 1.2.

## Adapted from Zepeda and Lanoue (2017)

Debriefing about what was observed is the conversation. Together, the coach and the principal analyze data collected during the observations. They identify common threads across all the classrooms related to the focus. The debriefing is professional learning related to

- pinpointing broad takeaways from the experience;
- modeling and rehearsing the "types" of conversations the principal would have with teachers;

Table 1.2 Conversation Walk Protocol

| Steps | Description |
| --- | --- |
| 1. Getting started: Initial meeting to develop a shared focus for the series of conversation walks | The principal and colleague (coach, fellow principal in the system, central office supervisor) meet to develop (1) focus of the observations (e.g., student engagement, etc.); (2) the length of each observation; (3) determine a system for the observations (e.g., grade level, subject area, teachers). |
| 2. Observe in classrooms | Both the principal and the coach observe teachers for a set period of time; take classroom notes about what is being observed related to the agreed-upon focus. |
| 3. Debrief | The principal and the coach review notes from each class observed and engage in conversations with each other. |

- bantering questions about teaching and learning in the context of classrooms, the work teachers do, and the focus for future principal development in these areas.

To drill into the events of the instruction that occurred in each classroom, the coach and the principal could identify two takeaways about each teacher's instruction related to the focus area that was mutually agreed upon in the first step, getting started. Some overall questions could be patterned this way:

- What data supports each takeaway and how would you describe what you saw?
- How would you start the conversation with the teacher?
- How would you link what was observed to targeted professional development for and with the teacher(s)?

These questions are just a starting point for the coach and the principal. The value of conversation walks is that they provide the opportunity for principals to engage in talking about instruction. Through role reversal, the coach and the principal can approximate what a conversation would look and sound like between the principal and the teachers that were observed.

Conversation walks can provide opportunities to extend reflection, inquiry, and conversations—the cornerstones to professional learning that is embedded in the work of leading, especially the instructional program and its relationship to developing capacity. Through professional conversations, leaders build a culture of learning. To build a culture of learning, leaders must have the skills to carry forward conversations in ways that support their own growth and the growth of others.

Conversations also serve to promote reflection. By taking purposeful pauses, leaders in the company of a coach can reflect on and make sense of the complexities of the classroom and the impact that instructional efforts have on students. More importantly, principals can begin to formulate short and long-term plans about the types of support teachers need to build their capacity as leaders in the classroom. For leaders, conversations through these walks help to cultivate expertise. Purposeful and targeted conversations help leaders to build their skill sets and the confidence levels as the lead learners in their buildings.

## MAKING SYSTEM-WIDE COMMITMENTS

Although principals need to be opportunistic about their own learning, they need district-level support. Districts that promote the active learning of their school leaders support skill development through coaching, engaging in conversation walks, action research, and other job-embedded learning opportunities. Strategic coordination of efforts helps to promote coherence of system initiatives with the work of leading these efforts at the site level.

System-level leaders engage principals in learning to lead by purposefully aligning long-term and sustained opportunities to the strategic direction of the system and to the needs of the context of individual schools. By focusing attention on what's needed at individual school sites, systems build the capacity of their leaders. If professional learning for principals is not systematic and part of the overall vision for the district, such efforts will not fully support the learning needs of its leaders.

## SUMMARY

As principals seek professional development to increase their own capacity and that of their schools, they need to actively make sense of what they are learning from their work and the professional development they need to extend their practices within the context of their schools. Regardless of their pathways to principalship, school leaders must understand that learning to lead is an ever-changing and long-term proposition that cannot be achieved through one-day workshops. As such, principal professional development should serve as a support system to address learning across their careers.

As illustrated in table 1.1, effective principal professional development practices are structured through five core features that are content-focused, hands-on, coherent with each other, ongoing throughout the principal career continuum, and collective. In addition to the prescribed quality features for professional development practices, to be effective and persistent in practice, principals should focus on their own professional learning through reflection and inquiry and conversations as the cornerstones of any professional development endeavor.

In this chapter, promising formal and informal principal professional development practices centered on reflection and inquiry and conversations are examined as the core features of the promising practices offered. These promising practices are categorized under four broad concepts: coaching, virtual spaces and social networks, action research, and conversation walks. Overall, this chapter provides a general description of promising practices for principal professional development and a roadmap for principals on how to transfer their professional learning into their leadership practices.

## QUESTIONS FOR REFLECTION

1. Can you describe the nature of your previous professional development experiences compared with the five core features of professional development?
2. As a sitting or aspiring principal, how do you feel about your ability to lead your own learning?
3. What does the leader support system look like in your current district?
4. After reading this chapter, what kind of changes do you want to make for your own professional development?

## REFERENCES

Aguilar, E. (2013). *The art of coaching: Effective strategies for school transformation.* John Wiley & Sons, Inc.

Allen, J. G., & Weaver, R. L. (2014). Learning to lead: The professional development needs of assistant principals. *Education Leadership Review*, *15*(2), 14–32. https://files.eric.ed.gov/fulltext/EJ1105575.pdf

Barnett, B. G., Shoho, A. R., & Okilwa, N. S. A. (2017). Assistant principals' perceptions of meaningful mentoring and professional development opportunities. *International Journal of Mentoring and Coaching in Education*, *6*(4), 285–301. https://doi.org/10.1108/IJMCE-02-2017-0013

Bengtson, E., Zepeda, S. J., & Parylo, O. (2013). School systems' practices of controlling socialization during principal succession: Looking through the lens of an organizational socialization theory. *Educational Management, Administration & Leadership*, *41*(2), 143–164. https://doi.org/10.1177/1741143212468344

Bold, C. (2011). Transforming practice through critical reflection. In C. Bold (Ed.), *Supporting learning and teaching* (2nd ed., pp. 189–202). Routledge.

Cheliotes, L. M. G., & Reilly, M. F. (2012). *Opening the door to coaching conversations.* Corwin Press.

Coghlan, D. (2019). *Doing action research in your own organization* (5th ed.). Sage.

Darling-Hammond, L., Hyler, M. E., & Gardner, M. (2017). *Effective teacher professional development.* Learning Policy Institute. https://learningpolicyinstitute.org/product/effective-teacher-professional-developmentreport

De Voto, C., & Reedy, M. A. (2019). Are states under ESSA prioritizing education leadership to improve schools? *Journal of Research on Leadership Education*, *16*(3), 175–199. https://doi.org/10.1177/1942775119890637

DeMatthews, D. E. (2014). How to improve curriculum leadership: Integrating leadership theory and management strategies. *The Clearing House: A Journal of Educational Strategies*, *87*(5), 192–196. https://doi.org/10.1080/00098655.2014.911141

Desimone, L. M. (2011a). A primer on effective professional development. *Phi Delta Kappan, 92*(6), 68–71. https://doi.org/10.1177/003172171109200616

Desimone, L. M. (2011b). Outcomes: Content-focused learning improves teacher practice and student results. *Journal of Staff Development, 32*(4), 63–68. https://learningforward.org/jsd/

Desimone, L. M., & Garet, M. (2015). Best practices in teachers' professional development in the United States. *Psychology, Society and Education, 7*(3), 252–263. https://doi.org/10.25115/psye.v7i3.515

Gerber, H. R., Abrams, S. S., Curwood, J. S., & Magnifico, A. M. (2016). *Conducting qualitative research of learning in online spaces*. Sage Publications.

Glanz, J. (2014). *Action research: An educational leader's guide to school improvement*. Rowman & Littlefield.

Goldring, E., Grissom, J. A., Rubin, M., Rogers, L. K., Neel, M., & Clark, M. A. (2018). *A new role emerges for principal supervisors: Evidence from six districts in the principal supervisor initiative*. Mathematica Policy Research, Inc. https://eric.ed.gov/?id=ED589024

Goldring, E., Rubin, M., & Herrmann, M. (2021). *The role of assistant principals: Evidence and insights for advancing school leadership*. The Wallace Foundation. https://www.wallacefoundation.org/knowledge-center/pages/the-role-of-assistant-principals-evidence-insights-for-advancing-school-leadership.aspx

Gordon, S. P. (2020). The principal development pipeline: A call for collaboration. *NASSP Bulletin, 104*(2), 61–84. https://doi.org/10.1177/0192636520923404

Gumus, E., & Bellibas, M. S. (2016). The effects of professional development activities on principals' perceived instructional leadership practices: Multi-country data analysis using TALIS 2013. *Educational Studies, 42*(3), 287–301. https://doi.org/10.1080/03055698.2016.1172958

Gurley, D. K., Anast-May, L., & Lee, H. T. (2015). Developing instructional leaders through assistant principals' academy: A partnership for success. *Education and Urban Society, 47*(2), 207–241. https://doi.org/10.1177/0013124513495272

Hallinger, P., & Bridges, E. M. (2017). A systematic review of research on the use of problem-based learning in the preparation and development of school leaders. *Educational Administration Quarterly, 53*(2), 255–288. https://doi.org/10.1177/0013161X16659347

Hallinger, P., & Murphy, J. F. (2012). Running on empty? Finding time and capacity to lead learning. *NASSP Bulletin, 97*(1), 5–21. https://doi.org/10.1177/0192636512469288

Hitt, D. H., & Player, D. W. (2018). Identifying and predicting effective leader practices: Examining principal experience and prior roles. *Leadership and Policy in Schools, 18*(1), 97–116. https://doi.org/10.1080/15700763.2017.1384502

Honig, M. I., Copland, M. A., Rainey, L., Lorton, J. A., & Newton, M. (2010). *Central office transformation for district-wide teaching and learning improvement*. Center for the Study of Teaching and Policy. https://eric.ed.gov/?id=ED517767

Honig, M. I., & Rainey, L. R. (2014). Central office leadership in principal professional learning communities: The practice beneath the policy. *Teachers College Record, 116*(4), 1–48. https://www.tcrecord.org/

Jones, R. J., Woods, S. A., & Guillaume, Y. R. (2016). The effectiveness of workplace coaching: A meta-analysis of learning and performance outcomes from coaching. *Journal of Occupational and Organizational Psychology*, *89*(2), 249–277. https://doi.org/10.1111/joop.12119

Joyce, B., & Showers, B. (1982). The coaching of teaching. *Educational Leadership*, *40*(2), 4–10. https://www.ascd.org/el

Kanokorn, S., Pongtorn, P., & Ngang, T. K. (2014). Collaborative action professional development of school principals. *Procedia-Social and Behavioral Sciences*, *116*, 77–81. https://doi.org/10.1016/j.sbspro.2014.01.171

Kempa, R., Ulorlo, M., & Wenno, I. (2017). Effectiveness leadership of principal. *International Journal of Evaluation and Research in Education*, *6*(4), 306–311. https://eric.ed.gov/?id=EJ1166878

Lanoue, P. D., & Zepeda, S. J. (2018). *The emerging work of today's superintendent: Leading schools and communities to educate all children*. Rowman & Littlefield.

Leithwood, K., Sun, J., & McCullough, C. (2019). How school districts influence student achievement. *Journal of Educational Administration*, *57*(5), 519–539. https://doi.org/10.1108/JEA-09-2018-0175

Levin, S., & Bradley, K. (2019). *Understanding and addressing principal turnover—A review of the research*. Learning Policy Institute.

Levin, S., Leung, M., Edgerton, A. K., & Scott, C. (2020). *Elementary school principals' professional learning: Current status and future needs*. Learning Policy Institute. http://learningpolicyinstitute.org/product/professional-learning-principals

Liang, J., & Augustine-Shaw, D. (2016). Mentoring and induction for new assistant principals: The Kansas Educational Leadership Institute. *International Journal of Mentoring and Coaching in Education*, *5*(3), 221–238. https://doi.org/10.1108/IJMCE-05-2016-0044

Marshall, C., & Hooley, R. M. (2006). *The assistant principal: Leadership choices and challenges*. Corwin Press.

Master, B. K., Steiner, E. D., Doss, C. J., & Acheson-Field, H. (2020). *How can assistant principals be trained as instructional leaders? Insights from the PLUS Program*. RAND Corporation. https://www.rand.org/pubs/research_briefs/RBA255-1.html

Mestry. (2017). Empowering principals to lead and manage public school effectively in the 21st century. *South African Journal of Education*, *37*(1), 1–11. https://hdl.handle.net/10520/EJC-5cda88587

National Association of Secondary Principals. (2017). *Position statement: Principal shortage*. https://www.nassp.org/principal-shortage/

Pariente, N., & Tubin, D. (2021). Novice principal mentoring and professional development. *International Journal of Mentoring and Coaching in Education*, *10*(3), 370–386. https://doi.org/10.1108/IJMCE-01-2021-0015

Parylo, O., & Zepeda, S. J., (2015). Connecting principal succession and professional learning: A cross-case analysis. *Journal of School Leadership*, *25*(5), 940–968. https://doi.org/10.1177/105268461502500506

Parylo, O., Zepeda, S. J., & Bengtson, E. (2013). Career paths in educational leadership: Examining principals' narratives. *Alberta Journal of Educational Research*, *58*(4), 565–599. http://www.ajer.ca/

Psencik, K., & Brown, F. (2018). Learning to lead: Districts collaborate to strengthen principal practices. *Learning Professional, 39*(3), 48–53. https://learningforward.org/journal/june-2018-vol-38-no-3/learning-to-lead-districts-collaborate-to-strengthen-principal-practices/

Rogers, L. K., & VanGronigen, B. A. (2021). Beyond preparation: State approaches to early career principal induction. *Leadership and Policy in Schools*, 1–25. https://doi.org/10.1080/15700763.2021.1977333

Rowland, C. (2017). *Principal professional development: New opportunities for a renewed state focus*. Education Policy Center, American Institutes for Research.

Schön, D. (1987). *Educating the reflective practitioner: Toward a new design for teaching and learning in the professions*. Jossey-Bass.

Turnbull, B. J., Riley, D. L., & MacFarlane, J. R. (2015). Districts taking charge of the principal pipeline. Building a stronger principalship: Volume 3. *Policy Studies Associates, Inc.* https://eric.ed.gov/?id=ED555869

U.S. Department of Education. (2020). *Staff employed in public elementary and secondary school systems, by type of assignment: Selected years, 1949–50 through fall 2018*. https://nces.ed.gov/programs/digest/d20/tables/dt20_213.10.asp

vanNieuwerburgh, C. (Ed.) (2012). *Coaching in education: Getting better results for students, educators and parents*. Karnac.

Westberry, L. A. (2020). *Putting the pieces together: A systems approach to school leadership*. Rowman & Littlefield.

Westberry, L. A., & Horner, T. (2022, in-press). Best practices in principal professional development. *AASA Journal of Scholarship and Practice*.

Wise, D., & Cavazos, B. (2017). Leadership coaching for principals: A national study. *Mentoring & Tutoring: Partnership in Learning, 25*(2), 223–245. https://doi.org/10.1080/13611267.2017.1327690

Zepeda, S. J. (2015). *Job-embedded professional development: Support, collaboration, and learning in schools*. Routledge.

Zepeda, S. J. (2019). *Professional development: What works* (3rd ed.). Routledge.

Zepeda, S. J., Derrington, M. L, & Lanoue, P. D. (2021). *Developing the organizational culture of the central office: Collaboration, connectivity, and coherence*. Routledge.

Zepeda, S. J., Goff, L., & Steele, S. (2019). *C.R.A.F.T. conversations for teacher growth: How to build bridges and cultivate expertise*. Association of Supervision and Curriculum Development.

Zepeda, S. J., Jimenez, A., & Lanoue, P. D. (2015). New practices for a new day: Principal professional development to support learning cultures in schools. *Learning Landscapes, 9*(1), 303–319.

Zepeda, S. J., & Lanoue, P. D. (2017). Conversation walks: Improving instructional leadership. *Educational Leadership, 74*(8), 58–61. https://www.ascd.org

Zepeda, S. J., Parylo, O., & Klar, H. W. (2017). Educational leadership for teaching and learning. In D. Waite and I. Bogotch (Eds.), *International handbook of educational leadership* (pp. 227–252). Blackwell/John Wiley & Sons.

*Chapter 2*

# Communities of Practice

## *Leading Schools in the Twenty-First Century*

### R. Stewart Mayers and Jennifer Anderson

### INTRODUCTION

Today's school leaders face unprecedented challenges. Ambiguity, change, and new demands are only a few of the challenges faced by school leaders. In such times, school leaders must provide direction, remain focused, and adapt their practices, at times at a moment's notice, and still be resilient, positive, and visionary leaders. Zepeda and Lanoue (2021) describe the effects of stressful times on school leaders: "Superintendents and school leaders have the added responsibilities of navigating the unknown as the pressures mount to balance the best safety decisions with the best education decisions" (p. 14).

Every constituency of America's public schools has encountered uncharted waters. In today's world, students experience isolation, and teachers are challenged to devise new routines when ones that had seemed so common and dependable no longer exist. Parents are forced to find a balance between overseeing the safety and education needs of their children with the necessity of generating enough income to provide for their needs (Zepeda & Lanoue, 2021).

These new challenges have presented themselves against the backdrop of many of the more customary ones school leaders face daily. Teachers not only still seek professional learning to improve their practices, but they also need to learn new strategies and technologies as more often learning takes place in the virtual environment. Logically, administrators need to find new strategies to provide the support they, teachers, and staff need to successfully navigate these new learning challenges. Developing a community of practice is a strategy that is particularly well suited for preparing school leaders to successfully navigate today's challenges.

## What Constitutes a Community of Practice?

Communities of practice are dynamic, active learning societies designed to solve complex problems and generate solutions, to allow members to exchange ideas and share resources, and to create innovative approaches to real challenges. Educational communities of practice, where members have a shared identity, allow community members to learn from each other, build trusted relationships, pool knowledge and expertise together for the mutual benefit of members and their organizations, impact educational outcomes and school improvement, and transform systems and opportunities.

Wenger et al. (2002, as cited in Alkaher & Avissar, 2018) define communities of practice as "groups of people who share a concern, a set of problems, or a passion about a topic, and who deepen their knowledge and expertise in this area by interacting on an ongoing basis" (p. 494). Impactful communities of practice are highly collaborative and communal because members have a responsibility to build capacity in each other, openly share knowledge, and strengthen the organization or field.

Wenger and Wenger-Trayner (2015) believe that "communities of practice are formed by people who engage in a process of collective learning in a shared domain of human endeavor" (p. 1). Cashman et al. (2007), note:

> This definition allows for, but does not assume, intentionality: learning can be the reason the community comes together or an incidental outcome of members' interactions. Not everything called a community is a community of practice. A neighborhood for instance, is often called a community, but is usually not a community of practice. (p. 2)

This definition serves to remind that communities of practice are based on collective knowledge, experience, and expertise. They are thoughtful, with a distinct purpose to bring people together for a united cause and are far more than meetings and professional development sessions.

Saint-Onge and Wallace (2003, as cited in Li, Grimshaw, and Nielsen) described communities of practice as having three distinct components: people (who are involved in the community), practice (how the community operates), and capabilities (the ability to make an impact). These components merge to form the membership, function, and impact of the community.

Wenger et al. (2002, as cited in Li et al., 2009) describe three necessary characteristics found in communities of practice which they outline as domain, community, and practice. Domain is the bond or relationship between members of the community and how members interact with each other. Community refers to the learning group and the experiences it creates. Practice is the way ideas, lessons learned, reflections, solutions, and critical questions are shared.

Wenger et al. (2002, as cited in Li et. al.) believe that "successful communities offer the familiar comforts of a hometown, but they also have enough interesting and varied events to keep new ideas and new people cycling into the community" (p. 6). Wenger and Wenger-Trayner (2015) explain that "familiarity in these events create a comfort level that invites candid discussions" and that communities of practice "develop a shared repertoire of resources, experiences, stories, tools, ways of addressing recurring problems in short, a shared practice. This takes time and sustained interaction" (p. 2).

According to Wenger (1998), a community of practice significantly differs from a team in that "the shared learning and interest of its members are what keep it together. It is defined by knowledge rather than by task and exists because participation has value to its members" (p.4). Furthermore, he contends that communities of practice are distinct from professional networks because networks are simply about relationships and communities of practice are about something deeper.

Bryk et al. (2015) assert that networked professional communities accelerate learning of all the community's members and they argue that such communities support teamwork and a sense of shared accomplishment. The ability of community members to come together and address the challenges and complexities associated with leadership reinforce a sense of team. The sense of team, building synergy, and the notion that together we can do "this" is the outcome of a highly functioning community of practice.

Wegner (1998) details that a community of practice exists because "it produces a shared practice as members engage in a collective process of learning" (p.4) and emphasizes that "communities of practice develop around things that matter to people. As a result, their practices reflect the members' own understanding of what is important" (p. 2). According to Wegner, communities of practice take ownership of their responses to outside influences: "Even when a community's actions conform to an external mandate, it is the community—not the mandate—that produces the practice" (p. 2).

## Merits of Communities of Practice

The Bastow Institute of Educational Leadership (2019) notes, "The best education systems in the world are highly networked. These systems have principals who are well-connected to their peers through active partnerships and learning networks" (para. 1). The Center for State, Tribal, Local, and Territorial Support (2015) maintains that both organizations and individual communities of practice members benefit from participation in communities of practice.

Lortie (1975) identified isolation as a major challenge for many teachers. In too many cases, classrooms act as silos, keeping teachers apart. Beginning teachers, in particular, feel compelled to look inward for solutions to the problems of practice: "Because of his isolation the beginning teacher frequently workings things out as best he can before asking for assistance" (p. 73). Building sufficient trust for teachers to share their challenges with each other or school leaders, is a common function of a community of practice.

This support is helpful for all teachers and school administrators, not just the beginner. Some benefits for organizations and school districts include the removal of learning silos, reduction of learning curves, dissemination of knowledge, and coordination of efforts across organizations, as well as innovation for problem-solving. Benefits for individual members include continuous learning, access to expertise, communication and relationship building, and a sense of professional identity.

According to Wenger and Wenger-Trayner (2015), "It may be difficult to attribute with 100% certainty the activities of a community of practice to a particular outcome" (p. 6). They argue that by using quantitative and qualitative data one can "measure different types of value created by the community and trace how members are changing their practice and improving performance as a result" (p. 6).

Wenger (1998, as cited in Lee et al., 2017) assert that "communities of practice are a force to be reckoned with" and contend that such communities act as "a locus of engagement in action, interpersonal relations, shared knowledge, and negotiation of enterprises, such communities hold the key to real transformation, the kind that has real effects on people's lives" (p.2). They further assert that "the influence of other forces (e.g., the control of an institution or the authority of an individual) is no less important, but they must be understood as mediated by the communities in which their meanings are to be negotiated in practice" (p. 2).

Communities of practice can be transformative and support the challenging work of school leadership when they are purposeful, solution-centered, rooted in shared values and trust, and focused on powerful outcomes. Their strength lies in the ability of the community to face, head-on, the innate challenges of school leadership.

## Building- and District-Level Communities of Practice

A community of practice is an outgrowth of the needs schools and school districts have to pursue innovation, engage in collaboration, solve complex problems, and grow leadership capacity. The Bastow Institute of Educational Leadership (2019) notes, "effective school networks, that are focused on collaborative effort to improve student outcomes, have rich conversations, use data for improvement and are powerful drivers of purposeful learning and leadership, can make a difference" (para. 1).

A community of practice at the individual school or building level can take many different forms and serve different purposes. An administrative team might form a community of practice to study new initiatives, examine best practices, make decisions about the daily leadership of a school, or analyze student learning outcomes. With this type of community of practice, no one person is in charge. It is vital that all members have equal voice to share ideas, identify challenges, and bring forward solutions.

A leadership-based community of practice could also extend beyond an individual school. A community of practice for school administrative or leadership teams could be inclusive of feeder schools or similar grade banded schools. The Bastow Institute of Educational Leadership (2019) notes that "collaboration between schools can improve both schools' performances more quickly than the national average. . . . The sharing of effort, knowledge and resources in the pursuit of shared goals plays a central role in the achievement of student learning outcomes and reducing inequality across educational systems" (para 5–7).

These types of communities of practice seek to use similarities between members to make change, resolve issues specific to these teams, and learn from colleagues who share students, subjects, or issues. They serve the purpose of bringing practitioners together to share practices that support educational improvement and professional growth among all members of the community.

A building-level community of practice could also be more inclusive and include other school leaders such a department heads, counselors, and teacher leaders. These types of comprehensive communities of practice allow for those in the building to form professional relationships with people across teams, grade levels, departments, and classrooms. This type of community of practice removes silos that create isolation for the members of the community and allows community members to learn from others.

One purpose of a building-level community of practice may be professional development centered around a need, common theme, emerging trend or practice, or specific school focus. A school or site-based community of practice may also be centered on areas of inquiry, interest, or problem-solving specific to a school. Communities of practice, at the school level, may also be developed around a school's improvement plan and goals.

School leaders should support the free flow of collaboration and problem-solving so that the community of practice can be defined and brought to life. With a school-based community of practice, the exchanging of ideas, professional collaboration, opportunities to engage in problem-solving, and sharing of leadership are targeted to the needs of a school and its members.

Such communities can change the culture of how issues are addressed, decisions are made, problems are solved, and people work together.

Similar to school-based communities of practice, communities of practice at the district level can be organized and developed to support central office leaders who might not always work across departments. They can also be organized across the different entities and schools that are part of a district, thus allowing central office leaders to work with building-level leaders on whole district initiatives and problem-solving. Zepeda et al. (2021) assert, "To focus an entire school district on learning requires leadership to be extended and expanded across the central office divisions" (p.44).

A community of practice might also be formed with other superintendents or district office leaders in similar roles across a state or a region in order to collaborate about specific issues, policies, shared experiences, and solutions that impact district operations and leaders at the district level. Such collaborative communities allow members to pull together to solve common problems, share ideas and resources, and engage in professional development specific to their leadership role or situation.

Whether at the building level, district level, across a region, or throughout a state, communities of practice can meet virtually or in person. Meeting virtually allows people who may not be geographically close to each other the opportunity to collaborate, develop new relationships and knowledge, and share success and lessons learned. With so many virtual meeting platforms, geography is no longer an issue that prohibits the meaningful development of or sustained engagement in a community of practice.

## HOW TO ESTABLISH A COMMUNITY OF PRACTICE

Establishing a community of practice requires patience, time, and persistence. Like all leadership endeavors, establishing a community of practice begins by building a culture of trust. Paliszkiewicz (2010), cited in Paliszkiewicz et al. (2015), defined trust as

> the belief that another party a) will not act in a way that is harmful to the trusting firm, b) will act in such a way that it is beneficial to the trusting firm, c) will act reliably, and d) will behave or respond in a predictable and mutually acceptable manner. (p. 20)

When leaders are trusted, members of the organization believe group performance is improved (Geier, 2016). As trust increases, members of a community of practice become more motivated to give their best efforts. Trust is also key to quality interactions between stakeholders. An important element required for the development of trust is cultivating a climate of respect. This means valuing each other and being invested in each other's success.

Establishing trust makes possible the next step in creating a community of practice: agreement on the central beliefs that inform the district and school's vision and mission. A vision statement describes the organization as its members believe it should be. Defining the central beliefs, and therefore the vision, requires stakeholders to be able to discuss freely personal beliefs and viewpoints, prerequisite to identifying points of agreement. Bryson (2004) asserts, "Clarifying purpose can eliminate a great deal of unnecessary conflict in an organization and can channel discussion and activity productively" (p. 38).

A mission describes in concrete terms what the community of practice plans to do and why. Nagy and Fawcett (n.d.) believe good mission statements share three elements. They are concise, outcome-oriented, and inclusive. Mission statements are customarily no more than a sentence or two and describe the specific aim of the organization, what outcomes the community of practice plans to achieve, and how. Inclusivity of mission means identifying the broad spectrum of strategies to be used and who will be involved.

With trust established, common beliefs identified, and a mission formulated, the school's and district's momentum must be maintained. This requires open, transparent communication, in both formal (meetings) and informal settings (communication in real time). Open communication allows all stakeholders to provide input on issues under discussion and for the free flow of important information.

Quality communication allows the members of a community of practice to connect to one another. In contrast to directive communication, connective communication fosters collaboration, improves listening skills, promotes feeling of partnership, creates an ethos of empowerment, increases understanding, and provides opportunities for asking needed questions. Furthermore, connective communication transforms the "my agenda" feel of top-down direction to belief that it is "our" agenda. Connective communication creates the climate where people are valued, listen to one another, take common ownership of the school's mission, and grow together (Maxwell, 2019).

Combined with trust, open communication provides the vehicle for members of the community of practice to take informed risks. When a community of practice becomes a community of informed risk takers, the ability to identify and solve problems rises to a higher level. Teachers and principals have the confidence to make professional decisions about the improvement in their practices. In turn, this creates a cohesive, connected team. Coherence and functionality in communities of practice result in "mutual accountability—in other words, taking joint responsibility" (Zepeda et al., 2021, p. 233) for each other's success.

The last step to developing a community of practice is nurturing the shift from "doing a job" to "fulfilling a calling" (Maxwell, 2019, pp. 236–237). Doing a job focuses on the important functions of earning a living and supporting one's family. These are, indeed, significant and necessary goals. For a community of practice, they are not enough. By shifting from a job to a calling, the professionals in a community of practice transition from a sole focus on themselves to a focus on the community. The belief in a calling permeates the entire being of community members. Success is measured by the significance of the work (Maxwell, 2019).

## HOW COMMUNITIES OF PRACTICE OPERATE: A CASE FROM THE FIELD

The Durant Independent School District serves a diverse student population of 3,478 in south-central Oklahoma. The district is led by Superintendent Duane Merideth and Assistant Superintendent Kenny Chaffin. It is comprised of one early childhood center, three elementary schools, an intermediate school, a middle school, a high school, and the Durant Vision Academy, a campus for students with significant challenges.

Major employers in the area include a large glass company, a steel mill, the Choctaw Nation, and Southeastern Oklahoma State University. The district's mascot is the lion. The district's philosophy is centered on the vision that "Once a Lion, Always a Lion." This vision illustrates the district's long-term commitment to its employees and students. It also indicates the belief the district is "one team" and "one family."

Building a community of practice began with the mission of "Reaching Every Student, Every Day, Every Way" and the realization there was more than one community of practice that needed to exist. The two communities became the community of practice in the district office and the community of practice comprised of the building principals and central office administrators.

Both communities of practice are centered on a single idea: trust. Nurturing trust is an everyday task. Building trust requires the district to hire the best staff for each position and then allow those hired to take responsibility for their work, trusting, respecting, and valuing them as professionals and providing them with the resources needed for success.

Also early in the process, the team needed to establish norms of communication and collaboration. Communication, both formal and informal, is critical to successful collaboration. Central office administrators meet with principals once per month. Meetings are focused, problem-solving events that are planned to respect the time of all involved. They are never "oral emails." Informal communication is also critical to building trust, maintaining connections, providing support, and for addressing specific issues in real time. As Superintendent Merideth said, "We meet once a month, but the phone lines are always open."

Building a community of practice in the district office was necessary to get support and resources to buildings and classrooms to properly equip students and staff for the teaching and learning process. This community of practice engages in continuous dialogue about the challenges identified at the building and classroom levels. These conversations occur in a safe environment that encourage risk-taking and innovation at the district office and beyond. This practice is supported by a third community of practice, the county superintendent group. These professionals meet once a month to exchange information, problem-solve, and share resources.

The Durant team continually returned to its mission of "Reaching Every Student, Every Day, Every Way." Being true to this mission required the district communities of practice to work each day to reinforce internally and externally what had become the norms of trust, respect, and valuing one another. This meant decisions being made at the classroom and building level by those closest to and most familiar with the needs. This realization necessitated the creation of a community of practice at each campus. Durant High School presents a particularly compelling story.

Ms. Cheryl Conditt has served as principal of Durant High School for twelve years. Building the community of practice at the high school followed a similar path to that blazed at the district level. After agreeing to "buy in" to the district's belief of "family first," the teachers and administrators began studying "High Schools that Work" research on best-practice first published by the Southern Regional Education Board in 1987 (SREB, 2020). This study identified key practices needed at the high school to promote the development of their community of practice. It also led to the realization the community of practice needed to change its focus from teacher behaviors to student outcomes and learning.

An important development in the process of building their community of practice, Durant High School created a "Guiding Coalition," a leadership team comprised of administrators, counselors, and department heads. Although email and face-to-face conversation provide quick, and when needed, "real time" communications, formal meetings of the Guiding Coalition provide a periodic opportunity to exchange information, identify problems or issues, and to brainstorm potential solutions. A prime example of an issue that required a solution was the need for teachers to be able to meet.

Principal Conditt asserts, "Do not require/ask teachers to meet without giving them the time to do so." This belief led to the creation of flexible

Fridays in which teachers report at the regular time, but students do not report until an hour later. This flex time allows teachers to discuss student issues, confer with counselors or administrators, and brainstorm problems of practice. Solutions are identified through examining student data, reviewing existing research, and consulting with communities of practices in other schools. Solutions are shared with building and district administration to appropriate resources and supports can be made available.

An issue identified through anecdotal data was the need to revamp how in-school suspension was used to address student behavior. In-school suspension practices were not providing students an opportunity to reflect on their behavior or why it is important to *not* be in in-school suspension. The DHS community of practice decided that, in addition to all regular academic work, students in in-school suspension would be required to complete projects to help them understand the consequences of their actions and the importance of changing behaviors. This solution to the ISS issue was created with assistance from another area high school.

Each day, the Durant ISD strives to be true to its mission to reach every student, every day, every way. This means continuous communication within and between the different communities of practice. It also means a constant commitment to openness, transparency, and service to all stakeholders. When the COVID pandemic hit in March 2020, Durant staff ended spring break early and began brainstorming all the ways the district needed to be prepared to serve students and their families. Commitment to a mission and beliefs requires all members to walk the walk.

## SUMMARY

Today's school leaders work in unprecedented times. World health crises, quickly evolving technology, open borders, students' social and emotional needs, teaching shortages, budgetary constraints, and emerging demands combine to elevate the stress levels of every member of the school community. There is also a need for leaders and teachers to examine their practices and grow their capacity to support student learning and growth, resulting in school improvement. Given these aforementioned complexities associated with education, communities of practice have a dynamic role to play in resolving new and ongoing systemic challenges.

According to Cambridge et al. (2005), while communities of practice require cultivation so that they can emerge and grow, it is ultimately "the members of the community who will define it and sustain it over time" (p. 1). Given this, districts and schools must provide the time for members to develop communities of practice in a way that allows the community to grow.

The sustained effort of community members to pull together knowledge, exchange ideas, and share success and lessons learned requires an investment of time, trust, synergy, and communication.

Leaders must give members time to engage in the community and to test solutions generated by community members. Members must utilize time wisely so that the community of practice can focus on the agreed-upon vision and mission of the community. Trust is the key element of a community of practice that allows members to be open, vulnerable, ask for support, and learn from mistakes. Establishing a shared purpose, vision, and mission is also vital if the community is to be impactful. Additionally, communication is a key factor in the ability of a community of practice to identify struggles, generate solutions, and nurture transparency and trust.

The work undertaken by school leaders has a profound impact on students, teachers, staff, schools, and communities. Because of the impact of teaching, learning, and leading on internal and external stakeholders, it is vital that members of communities of practice have opportunities to cross boundaries, get out of silos, and engage with others involved in similar practices. The important work of empowering leaders, teachers, and staff to create meaningful change, while supporting their professional development, must be a central component of a community of practice.

The demands placed on twenty-first-century schools require the kind of capacity expanding efforts envisioned by Bryk et al. (2015) that professional communities accelerate learning and "enliven a belief that we can accomplish more together that even the best of us can accomplish alone. A shared working history, common measures, and communication mechanisms anchor collective problem solving" (p. 173).

## QUESTIONS FOR REFLECTION

1. What are the paramount differences between Professional Learning Communities and Communities of Practice?
2. Zepeda et al. (2021, p. 233) contend that "mutual accountability—in other words, taking joint responsibility" for each other's success is integral in a community or practice. Why is mutual accountability for another's success so important in these communities?
3. Discuss ways a community of practice can actively identify problems of practice and find needed solutions in order to be part of the community and contribute to its strength and growth?
4. Why are vision and mission important to the creation and maintenance of a community of practice?

5. As you envision creating a community of practice in your workplace, what are some of the challenges you would expect to encounter? How would you meet those challenges? What topics would you anticipate addressing?

## REFERENCES

Alkahe, I., & Avissar, I. (2018). Assessing the impact of a program designed to develop sustainability leadership amongst staff members in higher education institutes: A case study from a community of practice perspective. *Environmental Education Research, 24*(4), 492–520. https://doi.org/10.1080/13504622.2017.1291799

Bastow Institute of Educational Leadership. (2019). *Communities of practice system leadership approach.* https://www.bastow.vic.edu.au/leadership-initiatives/communities-of-practice/communitiesof practice-system-leadership-approach

Bryk, A., Gomez, L., Grunow, A., & LeMahieu, P. (2015). *Learning to improve: How America's schools can get better at getting better.* Harvard Education Press.

Bryson, J. M. (2004). *Strategic planning for public and nonprofit organizations: A guide to strengthening and sustaining organizational achievement* (3rd ed.). Jossey-Bass.

Cambridge, D., Kaplan, S., & Suter, V. (2005). *Communities of practice design guide.* https://library.educause.edu/-/media/files/library/2005/1/nli0531-pdf.pdf.

Cashman, J., Linehan, P., & Rosser, M. (2007). *Communities of practice: A new approach to solving complex educational problems.* National Association of State Directors of Special Education.

Center for State, Tribal, Local, and Territorial. (2015). *Communities of practice resource kit.* United States Department of Health and Human Services. https://www.cdc.gov/phcommunities/resourcekit/intro/benefits_of_communiites of practice.html

Geier, M. T. (2016). Leadership in extreme contexts: Transformational leadership, performance beyond expectations? *Journal of Leadership & Organization Studies, 23*(3), 234–247.

Lee, Y., Chang, C., Chin, S., & Yoneda, F. (2017). Multicultural teacher education as a community of practice: M.Ed./PDS graduates' perceptions of their preparation to work with diverse students. *The Professional Educator, 42*(1). https://doi.org/10.1177/0022487114533386

Li, L. C., Grimshaw, J. M., Nielsen, C., Judd, M., Coyte, P. C., & Graham, I. D. (2009). Evolution of Wenger's concept of community of practice. *Implementation Science, 4*(1), 1–8.

Lortie, D. C. (1975). *School teacher: A sociological study.* University of Chicago Press.

Maxwell, J. C. (2019). *Leader shift: The 11 essential changes every leader must embrace.* Harper Collins.

Nagy, J., & Fawcett, S. B. (n.d.). *Proclaiming your dream: Developing vision and mission statements.* https://ctb.ku.edu/en/table-of-contents/structure/strategic-planning/vision-mission-statements/main

Paliszkiewicz, J., Goluchowski, J., & Koohang, A. (2015). Leadership, trust, and knowledge management in relation to organizational performance: Developing an instrument. *Online Journal of Applied Knowledge Management, 3*(2), 19–35.

Southern Regional Education Board. (2020). *High schools that work.* https://www.sreb.org/high-schools

Wenger, E. (1998). Communities of practice: Learning as a social system. *The Systems Thinker, 9*(5), 1–10. https://participativelearning.org/pluginfile.php/636/mod_resource/content/3/Learningasasocialsystem.pdf

Wenger, E., & Wenger-Trayner, B. (2015). *Communities of practice: A brief introduction.* Communities of Practice. https://wenger-trayner.com/wp-content/uploads/2015/04/07-Brief-introduction-to-communities-of-practice.pdf

Zepeda, S. J., Derrington, M. L., & Lanoue, P. D. (2021). *Developing the organizational culture of the central office: Collaboration, connectivity, and coherence.* Routledge.

Zepeda, S. J., & Lanoue, P. D. (2021). *A leadership guide to navigating the unknown in education: New narratives amid COVID-19.* Routledge.

*Chapter 3*

# Principal Mentoring as Professional Learning

Arvin D. Johnson

## INTRODUCTION

The principal is among the most influential people in a school and their role is critical to the overall school success (Grissom et al., 2015; Liebowitz & Porter, 2019). Principals have a direct impact on nearly every aspect of the school setting. This includes instructional leadership, climate and culture, facilities, human resources, decision-making, and many other areas. In addition, every school and district have several nuances that are specific to the setting. For example, the leadership demands at a rural middle school primarily serving students from low-income families may be distinctly different from a suburban or urban school.

Principals must provide overall leadership in many areas (Johnson, 2016). In addition, they must also be equipped to navigate increasingly complex schools. Schools have become more complex for many reasons (e.g., COVID-related changes, economic demands). Preparation for these complexities is not always black and white and often falls into the gray area. This means that principals may face situations that require problem-solving that was not included in their initial preparation; this is where mentoring can help. Principal mentoring can serve as an effective professional learning mechanism when implemented correctly (Bickmore & Davenport, 2019; Hayes, 2019).

Principals are leaving the profession at alarming rates for a variety of reasons (Gimbel & Kefor, 2018). The demands of the role, overall performance, burnout, preparation, and many other reasons may be potential causes (Yan, 2020). This chapter highlights various aspects of principal mentoring as professional development and learning. Mentoring may help curb the number of principals leaving the profession. These professional learning opportunities are extremely important considering that school leadership has a tremendous influence on the learning environment in schools (Babo & Petty, 2019; Day et al., 2020).

## PRINCIPAL PREPARATION

In most states, to become a principal, state boards of education require several levels of preparation (Davis et al., 2020). A master's degree in education leadership/administration or equivalent is typically required from an accredited university or other educational entity. A minimum of three years of teaching experience is a common requirement. An internship or residency/applications coursework is an additional requirement in most states. Only twenty states require some form of principal mentoring (Gimbel & Kefor, 2018; Spiro et al., 2007). Finally, passing some type of state examination is required for state certification.

Principal certification and access to principal pools vary by state and district (Gimbel & Kefor, 2018). Some districts require the completion of district-level leadership development programs for entry into the principal pool. Other states require the completion of state-level leadership preparations programs. These programs may be offered by state or state-approved educational agencies. This formal preparation represents the minimal preparation needed. As in any profession, when the demands change, principals need continued learning to support their leadership skills and abilities (Johnson, 2016). Accordingly, additional professional learning is warranted and needed.

Supporting principals through professional learning is critical, especially for new principals, as they typically do not have the experience and/or knowledge to be successful (Acton, 2021). Principals are typically charged with many tasks and must serve in several expanding roles (Bush, 2018). Often the roles and tasks of principals are challenging and time-consuming and may not leave much time for principals to reflect on their own professional learning needs (Levin et al., 2020). Consequently, those who supervise principals should actively attend to the needs of building the capacity of principals through professional learning.

## PRINCIPAL MENTORING

Principal mentoring can be used as a professional learning model for new and established principals (Sutcher et al., 2018). Principal mentoring involves the relationship between a less experienced principal (mentee) and a more experienced principal (mentor) (Lipke, 2020). Principal mentoring involves assigning a person with more experience, ability, and knowledge of the principalship as a mentor to newer principals. These mentors typically collaborate with new principals to assist in developing the skills needed to be successful in the role. Designing and implementing a principal mentoring program is a vehicle to develop and support principals.

## Establishing Mentoring Programs

Mentoring is used in many personal and professional settings for several reasons (Lefebvre et al., 2020). Mentoring provides a formal process for mentees to seek knowledge and confide in individuals with more experience (Hayes, 2019). District leaders are allowed to support principals by delegating principal mentoring assignments to actual principals rather than serving in these capacities. Mentoring can be used to teach some of the informal roles that principals must be able to lead and navigate. Finally, mentoring may help with principal attrition and success (Sutcher et al., 2018).

An effective principal mentoring program must be supported at multiple levels, starting with the superintendent. Support from the superintendent helps establish creditability, improves implementation, and ensures sustainability of the program. Associate superintendents/designees must be deeply involved in the process, as they typically serve as direct supporters/evaluators of principals. District superintendents in smaller school districts may have the capacity to lead a principal mentoring program. However, most will need to delegate and charge designees to develop, implement, and monitor the progress of such mentoring programs.

The first steps of establishing an effective principal mentoring program should begin with a review of pertinent data. The superintendent/designee should begin the process of assessing the needs of principals through a formal needs assessment. The data collected should help provide a framework for developing an effective principal mentoring program. This step is very important because it will identify the specific types of support needed for each school district. Each needs assessment will look different; however, there are some components that all should include.

An examination of the demographics of existing and aspiring principals may be a good starting point. These demographics will provide information on principal experience and readiness levels, and will serve to help categorize principals. District administrators could use demographic data to ascertain existing principals who are well-positioned to serve as mentors. In addition, demographic data will reveal the number of aspiring principals who are ready to transition into principalship. Examining the demographic data is highly informative.

A comprehensive review of principal attrition rates over the last few years will also provide valuable information. By reviewing principal attrition data, school district administrators can identify trends. Furthermore, the use of exit surveys can help district leaders identify the reasons principals leave. These data points help district leaders determine if attrition is due to retirement, burnout, performance issues, and/or other reasons. Equipped with this data, potential solutions can be interwoven into the planning of a principal mentoring program.

Principals serve in many roles; however, instructional leadership is among the most important (Leithwood et al., 2004). Accordingly, a multifaceted assessment of academic achievement data is recommended. This data will offer a snapshot of what type of instructional leadership is needed in the district. For example, historically low-performing schools will need a principal who has strong instructional leadership skills and/or the need for this mentoring will be highlighted. Data gained in this area can also inform district-wide priorities and highlight areas that may need to be a part of every principal's mentoring plan.

School-wide discipline data should be included in the district-level needs assessment. Effective school discipline impacts many other areas of the school. These areas may include student achievement, principal and teacher effectiveness, attrition, safety, and the overall learning environment. School discipline data can be used to inform the development of principal mentoring plans. Primarily by highlighting discipline trends at schools throughout the district, this data can be aligned to mentor expertise and strategically targeted in mentoring plans.

A review of school climate/culture data is informative to district leaders and can be insightful regarding providing support for principals. Most educators and scholars agree that school climate and culture are very important functions of schools as they impact the overall learning environment (Payne, 2018). By examining the results of the school climate/culture data, district leaders can determine some of the specific needs in schools. This data, in turn, should be used to ensure that several mechanisms are in place to support principals in this area. Also, district administrators may determine that other internal data points should be included in the needs assessment.

An examination of other principal mentoring programs can be useful to school district leaders. By examining mentoring programs used by school districts, leaders can gain ideas regarding new and innovative program designs. These ideas may be embedded in newly designed programs. Leaders may identify specific program elements that can be modified to align with the professional learning needs within their districts. In addition, an examination of other school district programs will help district administrators avoid "groupthink." Groupthink refers to the process of making decisions based on group consensus rather than exploring other alternatives (DiPillo, 2019).

Obtaining data through a principal focus group is another component of the needs assessment. District leaders should conduct one or more focus group meetings with existing successful principals. These individuals possess esoteric knowledge that can only be obtained through experience. District administrators should probe these principals to identify areas that should be included in the mentoring program. These topics may include, but are not limited to, the following: identifying areas in which principals struggle, the intersection between community and schools, what skills are most useful in the beginning years, and any other questions that may help in developing a comprehensive mentoring program.

## OPERATIONALIZING THE PROGRAM

After a needs assessment and internal/external data are collected and analyzed, it's time to construct the mentoring program. District leaders are cautioned not to take the formality out of this process (Spiro et al., 2007). An effective principal mentoring program should be written out in a manual-like document that provides a comprehensive description of the program. The components, structure, and guidelines of the program should be differentiated and transparent based on the needs assessment and data collection. Accordingly, every district program should be different; however, some components are necessary for all principal mentoring programs. See table 3.1 for recommendations for program development.

The needs assessment is developed at the onset of the program. This process allows district leaders an opportunity to gather and analyze pertinent information related to the specific needs of principals in the district. This information is then used to devise a principal mentoring program tailored to their specific school district. This step is critically important to ensuring the alignment of programmatic practices and data sets retrieved from the school district. The needs assessment is the foundation of the entire program, and considerable attention should be given to this part of the process.

Based on the needs assessment and input from key stakeholders (i.e., superintendents, regional/association superintendents, and experienced and

Table 3.1 Recommendations for Mentoring Program Development

| Components | Evaluation/Revisit |
|---|---|
| Needs Assessment | 1–2 years |
| Mission/Vision Statements | 3–5 years |
| Goals/Objectives | 1–2 years, based on needs assessment |
| Program Development | As needed |
| Program Evaluation | 1–2 years, based on needs assessment |

successful principals), the varying mission and vision of the principal mentoring program should be developed. The mission should focus on the purpose of the mentoring program (e.g., to build professional capacity within new/struggling principals, to develop principals with twenty-first-century skills). The vision should focus on the future direction for the principal mentoring program (e.g., to build a cache of well-prepared principals prepared to serve the district, to ensure principals are prepared to lead and function on the edge of innovative practice).

Using the needs assessment and mission/vision, district leaders can begin to develop programmatic goals and objectives. The goals should identify what are the overarching outcomes expected. Goals should be broader statements of what the program will accomplish. The objectives should be more task-specific and identify the strategies/activities that will be utilized to accomplish goals. These concepts also lay the foundation as metrics to determining program success.

An effective principal mentoring program must include an evaluation system that allows district administrators to assess the efficacy of the program. Reviewing program effectiveness data allows opportunities to reconcile gaps in practice and goals, redesign ineffective programmatic features, and continually improve the program. Evaluation procedures should be formal and will vary. District officials should spend considerable time exploring common program evaluation models (e.g., logic model, Kirkpatrick's (2016) four-level system) or developing an organic model. Evaluations of principal professional learning programs are warranted, effective, relevant, and should be timely (Bush, 2018).

## Program Infrastructure

How the mentorship relationship is operationalized becomes a crucial factor of success. Operationalization includes the formality of the mentorship relationship, frequency, platform of the interactions, accountability, and several other factors deemed important based on the needs assessment. School district administrators should give due diligence to the process of identifying and assigning effective mentors to new principals. Infrastructure details may vary, but all components should be included in the program manual and/or documentation. These details will solidify the structure of the program and allow for program sustainability that can be transferred as needed.

District leaders will need to determine the formality of the mentoring program and include this information in the program manual/documentation. Information must include the expectations of the mentor and mentee. As stated earlier, these expectations need to be concrete and clear. Potential mentor principals will need to refer to this documentation to help determine mentoring approaches. In the inchoate stages of development, district leaders need to specify the following:

A. What are the qualifications and how will mentor principals be selected? (Mentor Selection)
B. Which principals need mentoring (e.g., beginning, struggling, specialty areas)? (Mentee Selection)
C. How much time or how many hours of mentoring is required? How will it be tracked?
D. Who will develop and implement the mentoring program?
E. What are the outcomes of successfully mentoring and what will serve as documentation/evidence? (Program Evaluation)

## TYPES OF MENTORING

There are several types of mentoring that can be deployed based on the needs of the mentee(s) and the school district (Crisp, 2018). Mentors should use several variables (e.g., availability, distance, the safety of participants, the readiness of mentees, and other variables deemed appropriate) to determine which type of mentoring is most appropriate. In most cases, mentors should consider a variety of mentoring types. Three types of mentoring approaches are recommended. Goal-oriented, Skill-based, District-focus, School-type, Individual, virtual, small group mentoring are all applicable for principal mentoring. Each type of mentoring can be customized and used in tandem.

### Goal-Oriented Mentoring

Goal-oriented mentoring is a type of mentoring that involves developing goals based on the mentee's perceptions of their needs. The role of the mentor is to provide support to ensure that the goal(s) are viable and appropriate. Mentors should work to ensure that the integrity of the mentee's wish is upheld while making sure that the desired goal(s) applies to their role and success as principals. For example, a mentee may want to establish a better work-life balance. The mentor understands that this is a common experience of principals that can impact performance and principal efficacy. Now the mentor is better positioned to offer anecdotal strategies and help the mentee research other strategies.

### Skill-Based Mentoring

Skill-based mentoring involves the mentor and district administrators identifying specific skills that mentees need to improve. District administrators and mentor principals need to approach this type of mentoring by building upon the existing skill set of mentees. Identified deficits must be strategically addressed and developed; however, the approach should be based on the strengths of the mentee. For example, a beginning principal who does not spend enough time attending to instructional leadership but has great communication skills should have a plan to strengthen the mentee's instructional leadership skills and incorporate the mentee's communication skills.

## District-Focused Mentoring

District-focused mentoring is designed to ensure that certain skill sets are developed in all principals within a school district. The district priorities will vary, must be determined by school district administrators, and should be based on a comprehensive district needs assessment. A comprehensive review of the causes of principal attrition, student achievement, discipline, school climate, and principal perceptions provides the basis for developing three to five district principal professional learning priorities. These priorities lay the foundation for strategic district planning to ensure that all principals are well prepared in these identified areas.

Once these priorities are established, superintendents can charge assistant superintendents/designees to ensure that these priorities are included in principal professional learning. Superintendents/designees can also promulgate these priorities throughout the district to potentially prompt aspiring leaders to seek external avenues to gain knowledge in these areas. Assistant superintendents/designees should communicate these district priorities with mentor principals to ensure that they are intentionally embedded in all principal mentoring plans.

## Mentoring by School Type

Mentoring by school type is assigned based on the type of school that principals serve. This model is designed to ensure that mentee principals receive affiliated knowledge based on the type of school they serve. There are a variety of schools that fit into this category (e.g., elementary, middle, high, urban, suburban, rural, and specialty schools). Specialty schools (alternative, college preparatory, special needs, magnet, charter, Montessori, virtual, etc.) bring an added dimension. These schools require specificity in the way principals are prepared and mentored; preferably the idea is to align mentee principals with mentors who have successfully served in similar schools.

## Individual Mentoring

Individual mentoring is one-on-one mentoring. In this type of mentoring, primarily only two participants are involved—the mentor and the mentee principal. The conversations are confidential and provide a safe space for the mentee principal. In most individualized mentoring, the focus is on achieving goals, enhancing performance, developing a skill(s), and/or sharing effective strategies and problem-solving. The benefit of this type of mentoring is that it can build confidence, self-awareness, self-management, and skill development in a nonthreatening manner that focuses on the needs of the mentee. Mentees may be extricated from feelings of embarrassment based on ignorance.

## Small Group Mentoring

In small group mentoring, the mentor principal works with a group of one to six mentee principals. This type of mentoring is appropriate when mentee principals have similar needs or readiness levels. The mentor principal provides the goals, clarifies the roles and responsibilities, and helps the group develop purpose. Small group mentoring allows mentee principals to work with more mentee principals simultaneously, which can free some of the time restraints of individual mentoring. This type of mentoring offers flexibility and time-efficiency. One drawback of this model relates to exposing vulnerabilities; mentee principals may be reticent to expose their deficiencies in a group.

## Modalities of Mentoring

Virtual or in-person mentoring are viable options and may be used with different mentoring types. Virtual mentoring is delivered via a digital platform (e.g., Teams, Zoom, Google Meet, etc.). This delivery model has become very common recently due to a myriad of reasons (e.g., COVID, distance, and time restraints). The convenience of virtual mentoring offers a lot of benefits that face-to-face mentoring does not offer (i.e., no travel time, no exposure to unhealthy situations, convenience, and less costly to mentees or mentors); however, in-person mentoring offers a more personalized setting that may appear more intimate, authentic, and attentive than virtual.

## MENTORING AGREEMENTS

Mentoring agreements (Sample A), plan (Sample B), and log (Sample C) below should be developed based on mentee goals established, needs/goals of the school district, district-focused priorities, and school type. While there are no standard components for mentoring agreements and plans, both should be designed and implemented in collaboration with all stakeholders (i.e., superintendents/designees, and mentee/mentor principals) to ensure mentee success, support, and accountability.

These documents should be developed organically, or adaptations of plans readily available from multiple online sources. The goal is to ensure that mentee outcomes are identified, monitored, and measured systematically.

The mentoring agreement only needs to be completed at the beginning of the mentoring. The mentoring plan will need to be completed at the beginning and revisited throughout the process. The logs are designed to keep district administrators up-to-date on the activities and progress of the mentees. The samples included are only to be used as an example; district leaders and mentor principals are strongly encouraged to develop their personalized forms using this model or a different one. District administrators may consider developing these forms digitally for convenience and expediency.

Effectiveness should be monitored through evidence and/or documentation. The sample documents section above includes three documents (i.e., a mentoring agreement, plan, and log). These documents or variations of them may be used as documentation and ensure accountability among all stakeholders. The agreement should involve the mentee, mentor, and district administrator. The plan identifies the specific goals and provides evidence of progress at strategic points in the year. The log may be used to record mentoring sessions and activities. The log and the plan should be shared with district administrators periodically as an additional source of documentation.

## SAMPLE MENTORING DOCUMENTS

### Sample A

Sample Mentoring Agreement

Mentor _____
Mentee _____

This agreement between _____ (mentor) and mentee is effective on _____ and will continue for a period of _____. During this period, the mentee and mentor will participate in mentoring sessions for time periods to be determined by the mentee and mentor as aligned to the minimum number of hours needed to successfully complete the mentoring process _____ hrs.

The mentor agrees to:

a. Support the goals and objectives as stated in the mentee's mentoring plans

b. Share experiences and skills as deemed appropriately
  c. Collaborate with the mentee and superintendent/designee
  d. Maintain confidentiality of mentee progress
  e. Be available to support the mentee in impromptu situations
  f. Maintain and submit documentation/evidence of mentoring and progress

The mentee agrees to:

  a. Collaborate with the mentor to accomplish specified goals and objectives
  b. Fully participate in the established mentoring plans and meetings
  c. Seek assistance from the established mentor when needed

Mentoring may be provided individually, virtually, or in small groups via telephone, videoconferencing, or in face-to-face meetings as deemed appropriate by the mentor.

I approve this mentoring agreement as agreed upon all stakeholders (i.e., mentee, mentor, and district administrator).

_____ (mentee)      _____ (date)
_____ (mentor)      _____ (date)

## Sample B

Sample Mentoring Plan

| Mentor: | Mentee: |
|---|---|
| Duration: | District Supervisor: |

| Mentoring Goals | Date Met |
|---|---|
| 1. | |
| 2. | |
| 3. | |

## Progress Monitoring

Satisfactory—S, Needs Improvement—N

| Fall: |
|---|
| Spring: |
| Summer: |

| Reflections/Comments: |
|---|
|   |

| Next Steps: |
|---|
|   |

Mentee: _____ Date_____

Mentor: _____ Date_____

District Supervisor: _____ Date_____

## Sample C

Sample District Mentoring Report

Please submit one report per mentee periodically (i.e., fall, spring, summer) until the mentee has successfully met all mentoring goals. Include any impromptu or telephone meetings as well as normally scheduled meetings. Mentors, please submit your reports to the superintendent/designee.

| Mentor: | Mentee: |
|---|---|
| Duration: | District Supervisor: |

Mentoring Log:

| Session(s) | Timeframe | Format | Discussion/Activity |
|---|---|---|---|
| *(e.g.,. 2/12/22/12:30 PM)* | *1 hour* | *Individual Virtual* | *Goal # 2/Instructional Leadership* |
| | | | |
| | | | |
| | | | |
| | | | |
| | | | |
| | | | |
| | | | |
| | | | |
| | | | |
| | | | |
| | | | |
| | | | |

Mentor's Signature                                    Date

## PRINCIPAL MENTOR SELECTION

There are many factors for district leaders to consider when deciding who should serve as a principal mentor. Principal mentorship may be designed differently in many settings. However, an appropriate and authentic principal mentorship is an invaluable resource for aspiring and new principals. Principal mentors must be assigned strategically. Random and haphazard assignment of experienced principals as mentors may not produce desired outcomes and may be more detrimental than helpful. As a result, district leaders should investigate multiple factors when selecting mentors.

The selection of principal mentors will vary by district. Districts with several assistant superintendents overseeing principals may use these individuals to select mentors. Other districts may have one person who is charged with the overall principal leadership (e.g., directors of leadership), and mentor selection may be deferred to these individuals. If superintendents decide to delegate designing, overseeing, and maintaining principal mentoring programs, care must be taken to ensure their vision is thoroughly calibrated to designees.

Ultimately, superintendents assume the responsibility for the success and/or failure of principal professional learning. Therefore, district administrators must take considerable care when selecting mentor principals. Mentor principals should have adequate years of successful experience. Additionally, recently successful retired principals may serve as mentors.

A successful experience is important because it gives potential mentor principals the time and situational awareness to successfully navigate the myriad of circumstances that arise in the principalship. The diverse ways in which mentor principals have reconciled issues associated with the principalship makes them ideal candidates to provide support and guidance to less experienced principals.

There are some other qualifications that district administrators should consider when selecting mentor principals. The ability to build capacity in others is a necessity. Mentor principals must be able to be very supportive while holding others accountable. Another common characteristic of mentor principals should be a track record of effective performance evaluations. Other qualifications may include, but are not limited to,

- expert knowledge and skills in the areas of instructional and operational leadership
- the ability to build and maintain positive relationships at various levels
- effective decision-making skills
- the ability to think creatively and unconventionally
- expertise in other areas as deemed appropriate by district administrators

District officials must consider the current organizational demands of potential principal mentors. Some candidates may not have the capacity to mentor with fidelity based on their current setting. For example, a successful principal who was recently assigned to a high-needs low-performing school may not be best suited to serve as a mentor. There is no specific algorithm for making these types of determinations as they will vary by the school district. The underlying recommendation for district administrators is to consider the organizational demands of experienced principals before asking them to serve as mentor principals.

## MENTOR PREPARATION

For a principal mentoring program to be effective, there must be some written strategic goals/objectives associated with the mentoring process and the mentee. The goals/objectives should be based on district/school-determined needs. District administrators may determine that some mentees need several goals/objectives to be evaluated on a continuum, while others may only have one for the entire school year. The initial goals/objectives may be as simple as ensuring that the mentee develops skills to successfully navigate the first year of the principalship.

Selected mentors will need explicit professional learning to effectively serve (Crisp & Alvarado-Young, 2018). District administrators should determine the scope and depth of this professional learning. Minimally, a mentor orientation is needed to highlight expectations, purpose, and expected outcomes. During this orientation, mentors should receive details about their mentee assignment and information on how serving as a mentor will edify them as principal mentors. In addition, potential mentors must be afforded ample opportunities to ask clarifying questions to ensure they have a thorough understanding of the expectations of their roles.

## Monitoring Implementation

School district administrators should monitor the effectiveness of principal mentoring as a priority to support mentees and mentors. Monitoring mentoring plans should be a responsibility of all involved (i.e., the mentee, mentor, and district administrator). This inclusive model can help ensure overall accountability and adequate support. In addition, monitoring should be formative rather than summative. If any member believes more support is needed, that request should be revisited via the mentoring plan. This type of approach allows for ongoing modifications that make sense and are appropriate.

## Mentor Recruitment and Attrition

District administrators should develop a plan for mentor recruitment and attrition. Criterion-based recruitment can ensure all mentors meet specific criteria. However, administrators must understand that the role of mentor may be rewarding, but not all experienced principals will want to be mentors. Accordingly, ample effort should go into the recruitment, retention, and cycling of mentors. These efforts will help ensure an adequate pool of well-prepared mentors who are ready to serve and help develop capacity. Human and fiscal resources should be maximized to enable as many mentor principals as possible.

Although many principals may willingly serve as mentors, there should be some enticements to encourage experienced principals to serve. Enticements may come in a variety of forms (e.g., salary stipends, paid time off). Distinction classifications such as mentor principal and master principal could serve as an incentive to mentors. Such distinctions serve as recognition and public praise that principals may appreciate. District administrators should continually seek ways to support and reward mentor principals for accepting the task of mentoring others.

Recruitment of new mentors and the rotation of existing principal mentors should be systematic and intentional. Even the most effective and experienced principals may become burned out serving as principals and mentors. District administrators may safeguard against burnout by ensuring that principal mentor terms are limited and revolving. Other safeguards may include attention to the number of mentees, the needs of mentees, and the size of the mentors' administrative team. In addition, school district administrators must ensure that they showcase and promote the incentives of principal mentors to continually recruit potential new mentors.

## Mentee Selection

Multiple areas should be examined as district administrators determine who will receive principal mentoring. Ideally, all principals could benefit from some type of mentoring (e.g., professional learning, peer reflection, personal mentoring). However, many districts cannot provide mentors for all principals. Administrators will need to use specific metrics to help make this determination. Experience level, strengths, needed areas of growth, and other variables are factors for administrators to consider.

Principal mentoring serves as a viable way to build capacity in principals. However, the selection of mentees should be strategic and based on resources. Finally, school district administrators must consider district needs and resources to determine who will receive mentoring and identify the selection process.

## SUMMARY

Designing, implementing, and maintaining a principal mentoring program is a momentous task that requires a significant commitment. District administrators should ensure that significant time is allocated when the decision is made to engage in this process. Because the needs of individual school districts are diverse and complex, there is no perfect design.

Administrators can only ensure that programs are aligned to some common components and be intentional in design. Developing the correct components may ensure the needs of mentee principals and the school district are met. As with any program development, continuous review and improvements are needed for continued success and sustainability.

## QUESTIONS FOR REFLECTION

As school district administrators begin the process of developing an effective principal mentoring program, the following questions may offer some guidance throughout the process.

1. To what degree does the superintendent support a principal mentoring program?
2. Has the purpose, goals, and objectives been established for the principal mentoring program?
3. Has a design and implementation plan, to include responsibilities and a timeline, been developed?
4. How will mentor and mentee principals be selected?
5. How will the effectiveness of the program be evaluated?

## REFERENCES

Acton, K. S. (2021). School leaders as change agents: Do principals have the tools they need? *Management in Education*, *35*(1), 43–51.

Babo, G., & Petty, D. J. (2019). The influence of a principal's length of service and school socioeconomic classification on teacher retention rates in New Jersey middle schools. *Journal for Leadership and Instruction*, *18*(1), 8–11.

Bickmore, D. L., & Davenport, L. D. (2019). Principal transformative learning through mentoring aspiring administrators. *Mentoring & Tutoring: Partnership in Learning*, *27*(3), 235–250.

Bush, T. (2018). Preparation and induction for school principals: Global perspectives. *Management in Education*, *32*(2), 66–71.

Crisp, G., & Alvarado-Young, K. (2018). The role of mentoring in leadership development. *New Directions for Student Leadership*, *2018*(158), 37–47.

Davis, K., Rogers, D., & Harrigan, M. (2020). A review of state policies on principal professional development. *Education Policy Analysis Archives*, *28*(24), n24.

Day, C., Sammons, P., & Gorgen, K. (2020). Successful school leadership. *Education Development Trust*.

DiPillo, K. A. (2019). *Diversity, cohesion, and groupthink in higher education: Group characteristics and groupthink symptoms in student groups*. Youngstown State University.

Gimbel, P., & Kefor, K. (2018). Perceptions of a principal mentoring initiative. *NASSP Bulletin*, *102*(1), 22–37.

Grissom, J. A., Kalogrides, D., & Loeb, S. (2015). Using student test scores to measure principal performance. *Educational Evaluation and Policy Analysis*, *37*(1), 3–28.

Harvard Graduate School of Education. (2022). *The principals' center*. https://www.gse.harvard.edu/ppe/principals-center-programs.

Hayes, S. D. (2019). Using developmental relationships in mentoring to support novice principals as leaders of learning. *Mentoring & Tutoring: Partnership in Learning, 27*(2), 190–212.

Johnson, A. D. (2016). Principal perceptions of the effectiveness of university educational leadership preparation and professional learning. *NCPEA International Journal of Educational Leadership Preparation, 11*(1), 14.

Kirkpatrick, J., & Kirkpatrick, W. (2016). *Kirkpatrick's four levels of training evaluation*. ATD Press.

Lefebvre, J. S., Bloom, G. A., & Loughead, T. M. (2020). A citation network analysis of career mentoring across disciplines: A roadmap for mentoring research in sport. *Psychology of Sport and Exercise, 49*, 101676.

Levin, S., Leung, M., Edgerton, A. K., & Scott, C. (2020). *Elementary school principals' professional learning: Current status and future needs*. Learning Policy Institute.

Liebowitz, D. D., & Porter, L. (2019). The effect of principal behaviors on student, teacher, and school outcomes: A systematic review and meta-analysis of the empirical literature. *Review of Educational Research, 89*(5), 785–827.

Lipke, T. B. (2020). Leveraging a handbook for principal mentoring: Pathways in a district context. *Journal of School Leadership, 30*(1), 84–100.

Payne, A. A. (2018). *Creating and sustaining a positive and communal school climate: Contemporary research, present obstacles, and future directions*. National Institute of Justice Report.

Spiro, J., Mattis, M. C., & Mitgang, L. D. (2007). *Getting principal mentoring right: Lessons from the field*. The Wallace Foundation. https://www.wallacefoundation.org/knowledge-center/Documents/Getting-Principal-Mentoring-Right.pdf.

Sutcher, L., Podolsky, A., Kini, T., & Shields, P. M. (2018). Learning to lead: Understanding California's learning system for school and district leaders. Research Brief. Learning Policy Institute.

Yan, R. (2020). The influence of working conditions on principal turnover in K-12 public schools. *Educational Administration Quarterly, 56*(1), 89–122.

*Chapter 4*

# What Is the District's Role in Supporting the Principal?

Sherry Hoyle

## INTRODUCTION

Today's administrators are faced with ever-increasing demands from the federal, state, and local levels of governance. Calls for increased accountability requirements, heightened expectations of the public, student safety, and health concerns compound the challenges of the principal's job. In addition, the expectations of the role of the principal continue to morph from manager to instructional leader.

Although, in reality, practitioners recognize that the principal must wear both hats simultaneously. With the increased demands of accountability, along with the responsibility of managing a school, it becomes even more important for the superintendent and the district staff to maintain a high level of support for the building-level administrator.

## A SYSTEM APPROACH TO SUPPORTING THE PRINCIPAL

Key to defining the district role of the superintendent and district-level administrators is the need to ensure that there is a systems approach. Why is there a need for a system's approach? A systems approach is imperative if the goal is to establish a sustained system of support for principal leaders beyond the first year of the principalship and to yield a consistent workforce with minimal principal attrition. Systems thinking also provides a means of seeing the system as an integrated, complex composition of many interconnected components that need to work together in order for the whole to function successfully (Arnold & Wade, 2015).

By creating a leadership support system, internal and external resources are leveraged; these resources serve to not only lead to improvement at one school but also improve the whole system. Westberry (2020) noted, "The systems lens is the lens a principal must always look through in order to establish routines and process, answers questions, and create culture" (p. 7). The superintendent must utilize a similar systems lens at the district level when examining and evaluating the leadership support system.

This chapter will examine elements of the leadership support system, that is, high-quality mentoring/coaching for principals, professional development, and principal induction programs (PIPs). Each component will be defined and a description of what these elements look like at different stages of the principal's career (Bottoms & Schmidt-Davis, 2010).

Notably, the leadership needs of the novice principal will vary as compared to a principal in the latter stages of his/her career. Supporting and training administrators can occur through a variety of approaches. The adage "one size does not fit all" is accurate when a superintendent considers the varying needs of his/her administrators. Utilizing a tiered approach (see figure 4.1) provides flexibility within the leadership support system based on the stage of the administrators' career, that is, beginner, experienced, and so on, and also the flexibility to address any areas where the administrator may be struggling.

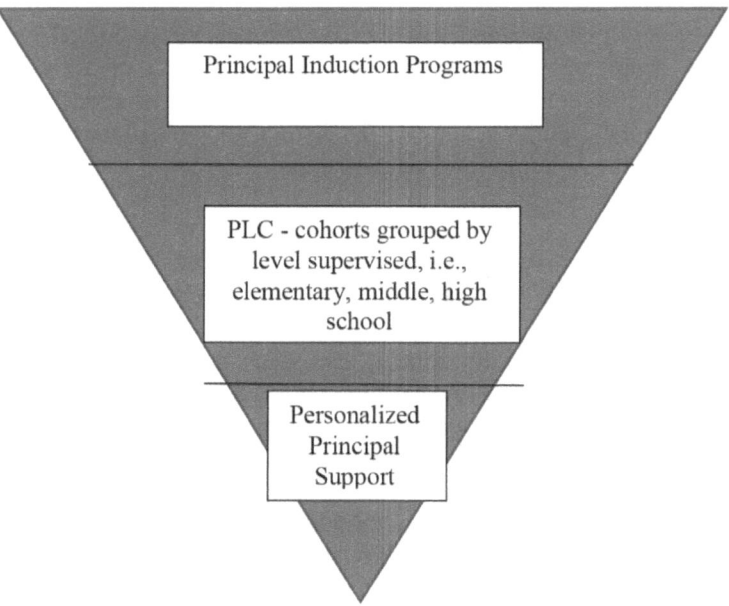

Figure 4.1 Tiered Principal Support.

## Principal Induction Programs

Principal/Assistant Principal Induction Programs (PIP) are typically utilized for onboarding administrators new to the position or to the school district. Interestingly, approximately one-half of state education agencies are mandated to facilitate an induction program for all new principals, with the remaining states deferring to the individual districts to create a new PIP (Rogers & VanGrongien, 2021).

In reviewing the induction literature, researchers identified five areas through which induction programs can support principal development:

1. building key leadership competencies and skills
2. coping with job stress
3. transmitting policy knowledge
4. lengthening tenure in school
5. deepening principals' professional networks (Rogers & VanGronigen, 2021, p. 5).

Wieczorek and Manard (2018) noted a number of areas in which novice principals faced challenges in management, leadership, people, and relationships. Interestingly, the identified areas do not highlight the need for development in instructional supervision, which highlights the transition from management to instructional leadership.

Although induction programs vary in terms of topic focus and duration, many programs are characterized by "a set of intensive experiences over a significant period of time, combining multiday retreats with daylong and partial-day experiences (Peterson, 2002, p. 230)." If a PIP is designed and executed effectively, it can reap great benefits for the school and the organization.

Wright et al. (as cited by Rogers & VanGronigen, 2021) maintained that an "area where induction plays an important role is helping facilitate principals' ability to build relationships with other principals in order to socialize into the role, collaborate, and seek advice" (p. 6). This cadre of professionals can serve as a great network of "think partners" when dealing with the demands and challenges of the job. What are the elements district leadership should consider when developing a PIP for principals?

1. What is the superintendent, district-level staff, and principals' vision of an effective PIP? What are the competencies that we want our administrators to possess? Engaged in this conversation should be stakeholders who supervise not only administrators but also several experienced administrators.

2. What is the timeframe of the PIP? Will it be a one or two-year induction program?
3. What will be the content of the PIP? What will be the expectations for how the content is delivered, that is, simulations, case studies, discussions, "a 'word' from the experts in the field," and so on?
4. How will the PIP work in tandem with principal mentors and coaches? How will the mentor or coach support the processing and implementation of the information addressed during the induction session(s)?

## Professional Learning Communities (PLC)—Level-Specific Groups

As administrators begin developing professional networks throughout the induction process, another approach is for the superintendent to provide opportunities for administrators to network within the grade span that is being supervised. The level-specific PLC affords administrators time to discuss similar challenges, common curricular goals, and so on, and create professional development opportunities in a setting where novice and experienced administrators can learn from each other. When asked, Heather, an eleven-year veteran principal, stated:

> I think we need time to come together . . . not to have another meeting to listen to a long list of things to do, but to have an opportunity to grow professionally and share ideas with each other in an atmosphere where we are not experiencing constant interruptions.

Experienced and novice principals do not want another meeting where professional development is one of the agenda items, and usually added to the end of the meeting. They want the opportunity to have uninterrupted time to discuss problems or issues, share best practices, and brainstorm ideas, learning from each other.

Ford et al. (2020) (as cited in Iatarola & Fruchter, 2004) purported that

> high-performing districts were differentiated from low-performing by the way they approached principal and school professional development. High-performing districts maintained a tight/loose balance, whereby they delivered highly conceptualized professional development. Instead of playing the role of provider, the district served more as a support resource for leaders in identifying, defining, organizing, and offering varieties of professional development opportunities. (p. 279–280)

What then can the superintendent do to support novice and veteran principals' professional growth? One way that district-level leadership can support professional development for the novice and veteran principal is by creating and facilitating opportunities for strategic networking through PLCs. The PLCs provide a forum for ongoing professional development, a more effective form of professional development than the one-day principal meeting format. The elements of the principal PLCs may include, but are not limited to, the following:

1. Time—The superintendent will support the allocation of a regular meeting time for the PLC.
2. Focus—The focus of the PLCs will be centered around a problem of practice, discussion of best practices, case studies, school visits, opportunity for reflection, and topics identified by the principals in the PLC (Honig & Rainey, 2014; Hord, 2009; Sutcher et al., 2017).
3. Role of the District—The role of the superintendent and district-level staff will offer support, such as time, resources, data to analyze problems, and other needs as identified by the PLC members (Sutcher et al., 2017; Hord, 2009).

## Personalized Principal Support—Mentor

This author questioned Holly, a veteran principal of four years, and she stated, "The first year of the principalship you observe and survive. Having a mentor helped to alleviate the stress of feeling like I was out there on my own." As noted previously in figure 4.1, the tiered approach to leadership support begins with a broad range of support through an induction program, progresses to more specific support/professional development through the level-specific PLC, and then narrows to how the superintendent and district-level leadership can more personalize the support for each administrator.

One approach for a more personalized approach can be accomplished through a mentor or coach. One of the most important decisions of the superintendency is the recruitment and hiring of principals (Saphier & Durkin, 2011). However, once the hiring is complete, the superintendent and district-level leadership must not assume that when the keys of the school building are handed to the new principal, he/she is automatically an expert and can be left primarily to his/her own devices. The superintendent and district-level staff must have a strategically defined program for mentoring the new principal.

Essential for every new principal in years one through four is the assignment of a mentor. A mentor must be experienced, must have a passion for the job, and must have the desire to "pay it forward" by mentoring the next generation of administrators (Grissom et al., 2021). A mentor serves as someone who provides a "sounding board," serves as a guide, and provides advisory support. In many districts, the mentor is a peer of the novice principal. What are the elements district leadership should consider when developing a mentor program for new principals?

1. What is the superintendent's vision for principal leadership in the district? The superintendent will facilitate the visioning process in collaboration with members of the senior-level leadership team.
2. What are the qualifications for the principal mentor? Is the principal mentor an exemplary administrator? Does he/she have a strong desire to mentor new principals? When selecting principal mentors, will the district utilize current practitioners, or retired principals? Will the district utilize district-level senior leadership to serve as principal mentors?
3. What will be the process for matching the principal mentor with the new principal, that is, match the mentor's administrative experience with similar school demographics as the principal (Sutcher et al., 2017)?
4. What will be the expectations of the principal mentor, and what type of in-service will be provided, that is, the superintendent's expectations; how often will the mentor work with the principal; how to support, not evaluate; how to coordinate efforts, and so on (Sutcher et al., 2017)?

After establishing the mentoring program based on these guidelines, there should be periodic "check-ins" with both the principal mentor and the principal to determine if the principal is receiving the support he or she needs. Simultaneously, the superintendent must also consider how to support continued growth of those who have progressed past the first years of the principalship.

In addition to utilizing mentoring and the PLC structure to provide a forum for principal conversation and professional development, the superintendent and district executive-level leadership must also create (implement) a more systemic strategy for providing targeted leadership development for principals who are in the experienced stage of their career and/or may be struggling in specific areas.

For administrators who need to "deepen their skills in specific areas" there are many opportunities that the administrator and the superintendent can consider for the personalized professional development support plan. Examples of ways to "personalize" the administrator's leadership support and professional development include, but are not limited to, the following:

1. attendance at national or state conferences (with the expectation that there is a "sharing" component, or implementation component to the activity)
2. advanced seminars offered through professional organizations

3. participation in professional reading and reflection groups of practice
4. book studies targeted at the identified area of growth (Peterson, 2002).

Of course, experienced administrators can also continue learning by becoming a mentor or coach. One school district designated time during the school day to focus on prioritizing professional development for administrators by organizing book clubs, biweekly meetings, and instructional rounds for administrators (Tew, 2019). One must also remember that district staff are also administrators and may need the same support to grow within their positions as well.

## Personalized Principal Support—Executive Coach and Professional Development

For those administrators who may need personalized leadership support based on an area(s) where they are struggling, it is vital to carefully consider the most effective and efficient strategies to employ in order to yield the most focused support and improvement efforts. One of the strategies for providing job-embedded, "just in time support," and personalized support germane to the principal's specific school-related issues is the opportunity to be paired with a principal/executive coach.

Farver and Holt (2015) in their study examining the value of coaching in building leadership capacity in urban schools asserted that

> the support of an assigned executive coach was beneficial in having a thinking partner available for goal-planning, action-planning, or solution-focused planning. As related to professional growth, participants in this study described leadership coaching as helping tremendously because it was job embedded work. (pp. 114–115)

A principal in the study commented (Farver & Holt 2015),

> Executive coaching gave me the opportunity to sit down and talk things over with someone. It gave me the opportunity to reflect with someone about practices. (The process includes the executive coach asking guiding questions.) Questions are asked that drill down deep and cause the [principal] to really get in touch with the true issue. Coaching is a safe place to do that, discuss your likenesses and concerns that are pretty serious. (p. 90)

The executive coach provides a different lens for principals as they process through issues and/or concerns. The utilization of executive coaching becomes another component of the system of support that provides the opportunity for consistent and sustainable professional growth for principals, in addition to the traditional methods of professional development, that is, national/state conferences, book studies, principal seminars, and so on. When a superintendent considers the idea of securing executive coaches for his/her principals, one must ask the distinction between assigning mentors versus coaches.

Based on Pelan's (2012) definition of the roles—"the coach-coachee relationship is a collaborative, a relationship of peers, and the mentor-mentee relationship is characterized by a more experienced person helping the less-experienced person with political advice, information and guidance" (pp. 35–36). Even though there are many similar skills shared by both the coach and mentor, the two deviate in areas such as the level of formality, with coaching being a more formal process, and mentoring being less formal and more likely a peer (Passmore, 2007).

Upon the superintendent's determination to move forward with employing executive coaches for principals, the superintendent and district leadership staff will first design the role and expectations for the executive coach. Following is a questioning framework that could be used to address planning when using executive coaches.

1. What is the superintendent's vision for coaching principal leadership in the district? The superintendent will facilitate the visioning process in collaboration with members of the senior-level leadership team.
2. What are the qualifications for the principal coach? When selecting principal coaches, will the district utilize external or internal coaches?
3. What will be the process for matching the coach with the new principal?
4. What will be the expectations/directed focus for the coach, that is, the superintendent's expectations; how often will the coach work with the principal; what will be the directed focus?

Having served as an executive coach for novice, as well as, veteran principals, this author has experienced first-hand the benefits, as cited earlier from the research, of utilizing executive coaching as a component of a school district's system of support for principals. The opportunity to develop a trusting relationship that establishes a shared commitment to professional growth results in providing "real time" support that reaps great dividends for the principal and ultimately the organization.

The rich conversations regarding issues wrapped around areas such as instruction, personnel, management, and even mental health regarding the stress of the administrator's role take on such an individualized approach. Notably, this author recognizes that the roles and responsibilities of the administrator are vast and complex, and not every area can be addressed.

## Building Trust and Relationships

The one consistent challenge, despite the years of experience, is building trust and relationships. What does the conversation between the executive coach and principal look like? What are the key areas that the executive coach and the principal need to collaboratively address? The conversation may be approached differently and tailored to the individual principal's school culture; however, the content or key conversation points to operationalize for improvement serve as the common focus and a guide for facilitative conversations between the executive coach and principal.

Most importantly, the executive coach will need to remind the principal that trust and relationships do not occur immediately but evolve over time. Below are specific behaviors identified by research that will promote/build trust. The key conversation points for the executive coach to facilitate with the principal should revolve around what these behaviors look like when operationalized in the principal's school.

As the executive coach facilitates conversations around how to build trust, there are key behaviors and/or practices the principal must engage in with his/her staff. According to Reeves et al. (as cited by Sinay et al., 2016), to enhance trust, administrators need to model respect and consistent support for teachers. According to Noonan et al. and Tschannen-Moran et al. (as cited by Sinay et al., 2016), open and clear communication and information sharing by the principal contribute to a positive climate of trust. Lastly, Noonan et al. (as cited by Sinay et al., 2016) maintain that transparency in decision-making instills trust among teachers.

It is not enough to acknowledge the behaviors and practices that enhance trust and build relationships, but it is essential for the principal to define those tangible actions that he/she will engage in on a daily basis with his/her staff. The executive coach can use the behaviors noted from the research as a springboard to facilitate conversation(s) that will lead the principal to engage in self-reflection and identify action steps, regarding the following:

1. Do the principal's daily actions (supporting teachers, open communication and sharing, transparency in decision-making) promote trust and relationship building? Make a list of the tangible actions you take.
2. If principal behaviors do not currently promote building trust and relationships in the areas mentioned above, what are those actions that need to be engaged in with the faculty that will promote trust. List specific measurable actions.

## Managing Time

Another area where administrators may struggle is with time management. When faced with the logistics of the day-to-day operations, unexpected conferences, scheduled observations, and drop-in visits from the superintendent or district-level leadership, the principal is bombarded with interruptions that impact the management of time. Shoho and Barnett (2010) maintained that "principals, are overwhelmed, specifically citing paperwork and time management as two areas contributing to the issue" (p. 568).

Respecting the fact that principals have their own unique style of managing time, how can the executive coach provide the support to facilitate discussion that will allow principals to reflect on how time is spent and assist in being a partner in brainstorming other ways to manage the work? Notably, the disclaimer for any discussion about time management and the principalship is that given the nature of the job, the best planned schedule can get sidelined with just one unexpected event that is presented. However, even given the potential unknown, it is better to have a system for managing time. Plans can be modified.

Another given is there are a plethora of time-management books, blogs, apps, and other resources to provide advice on how to best manage one's time. For example, one resource is Stephen Covey's book *First Things First* (1993) which states as time is prioritized consideration should be given to the fact that human resources in the organization are the top priority. Tasks should be prioritized in a way that would ensure the priority is on the people first as considerations are made for the daily/weekly "to do" list.

So, knowing that managing time effectively for the principal can be fluid based on the urgency of tasks that are presented on a daily basis, what are the key conversation points (between the executive coach and the principal) to operationalize for improvement if a principal is struggling with managing his/her time? Again, this is not an all-inclusive list; however, it will serve to direct the conversation.

1. What do you identify as your vision/mission that drives "what you do" and "why you do it"? What does your school need? How does knowing what your school needs aid in helping to prioritize your time? How do you prioritize based on identifying your vision/mission/purpose?
2. Keep a log or notes on your calendar for a designated period of time, that is, one week, two weeks, and so on. Engage in reflective discussion/thought. How did you spend your days? What are the daily tasks that had to occur? What are the tasks that demand large portions of your time? Are there tasks that are busy work that may demand your time, but are less important and can be completed in fifteen minutes or less?

3. Is there anything on the list of tasks that can be delegated to someone else? Will identifying blocks of time assist in providing windows of time for prioritizing certain tasks, that is, returning emails, completing reports, unplanned emergencies?
4. How do you schedule for ensuring you are visible in your building on a consistent basis?
5. Think about your most productive time(s) of the day. Do you feel you accomplish more in the morning? Afternoon? Do you need to focus on the most difficult task during the times you are most productive?

## Instructional Improvement

The demands on the roles and responsibilities of the principal to be a manager and instructional leader are ever increasing. How to accomplish improvement in the areas of curriculum, instruction, and assessment can be overwhelming for a principal who is struggling in any of these areas. Due to the interconnectedness of the three, it is important to recognize that a deficit in any one of the areas of curriculum, instruction, and assessment will impact the other.

Westberry (2020) in her work, *Putting the Pieces Together: A Systems Approach to School Leadership*, provides a great foundation and guideline for discussion and practice for the executive coach and the principal. Her approach addresses how to systemically look at curriculum and instruction and not just piecemeal improvement efforts. The trap for struggling administrators is having a myopic view of an instructional/assessment issue without digging down to discover the root cause of why the issue keeps occurring.

For example, one principal was puzzled about why students in grade 4 were consistently scoring low on reading benchmark tests. Was the issue student understanding, teacher instruction, the way the assessment was constructed, or alignment of the teaching of the standard and the manner in which it was assessed, and so on? As you can see, there are number of possible root causes as the principal drills down to the underlying issue(s). The approach of systemically looking at curriculum, instruction, and assessment provides a framework for principals to implement lasting improvements.

Therefore, if the focus is on taking a systemic approach, what are the key conversation points (between the executive coach and principal) to operationalize improvement if a principal is struggling with instructional improvements?

1. What is the identified area of need (discussion focus)? How do you know it is a need; that is, what data shows that the area identified for

improvement is the need? How do you determine the root cause of the issue?
2. Are your curriculum, instruction, and assessments aligned? How do you determine if there is alignment? What steps do you need to take? How do you prioritize first steps in the process for systemic improvement?
   **Refer to Westberry, L. (2020) *Putting the Pieces Together: A Systems Approach to School Leadership* to guide the conversation(s) for alignment, as well as provide examples of practical ways to approach the improvement efforts.**
3. How do you ensure that teachers have time for conversations that focus on how to align curriculum, instruction, and assessments for improvements, that is, teacher planning time, PLCs?
4. How do you schedule for teacher conversations and planning for improvements? Are current planning times sufficient? What are the current practice/administrator expectations during allotted teacher planning times? Are administrators present for teacher planning times, etc.? How is information shared?

## Managing Personnel and the Crucial Conversations

Effectively navigating crucial conversations can be challenging even for the most seasoned school veteran. What are ways to support the principals who struggle with having crucial conversations? From a district-level perspective, it is important for the superintendent to establish expectations for principals to address issues in a direct, yet respectful manner, while providing them practical guidance and tools for doing so.

One of the ways some districts provide a common set of expectations, guidance, and tools for conducting difficult conversations is to utilize the book, *Crucial Conversations Tools for Talking When the Stakes Are High*, by Patterson et al. (2002) for ongoing professional development. It is important to recognize that there are many resources on the market, and each district-level leadership can determine which resource best meets the needs of their district's vision and goals.

The key expectations and takeaways resulting in a common set of expectations, a consistent way to conduct the crucial conversation(s) and extensive opportunities for practice around the actual conversations that need to take place within the individual principal's building, serve to provide support for the principal. A report from the National Institute of Excellence in Teaching (NIET) (2021) maintains that "the role of district leadership in setting expectations and providing support for school leaders to create more effective professional learning and coaching systems in their school has been highlighted as the difference-maker" (p. 2).

What are the key conversation points for the executive coach to conduct with the principal if he/she is struggling with managing personnel and conducting the crucial conversation(s)?

1. What do you think is going to be difficult about the conversation; that is, will the conversation require a change in practice? Will the conversation impact evaluation ratings? Will the conversation result in a reprimand or personnel action?
2. Think about the key elements that need to be discussed during the crucial conversation. Utilize the coach as the thought partner for a different lens of the situation.
3. Don't forget to be an active listener.
4. Look at the situation from multiple perspectives—yours and the employee's.
5. Practice with the coach and actually role-play the conversation.

## SUMMARY

The type of district-level support for principals can vary based on the experience level of the principal. New principals need support navigating the waters of policies, procedures, protocols, and how to be an instructional leader. An effective new PIP and a high-quality mentoring program, designed by the district-level leadership, can serve to provide strategic support with just-in-time coaching.

Whereas the veteran principal may benefit more if the superintendent and staff provided time and resources for the principals to engage with peers in a PLC with parameters clearly defined by the superintendent. The principal PLC is designed to provide a fluid method of meeting the veteran principal's professional development needs.

In addition, a more personalized, job-embedded strategy for supporting principals from novice to experienced principal is the principal executive coach. By providing an executive coach, principals can receive a more individualized approach to professional development that happens in real time and is personalized based on the individual's current administrative assignment. In addition to personalized professional development, the executive coach can be instrumental in supporting improvement efforts if a principal is struggling in a particular area.

## QUESTIONS FOR REFLECTION

1. Does the district have a systemic approach to supporting the school-level leader?

2. What is the district vision for supporting the school-level leader from novice principal to career principal? If there is not a district vision, what should it be? How will the vision drive the work?
3. What elements are included in a systemic approach for providing support for struggling administrators?
4. What additional ways are there to provide personalized principal support for professional development?
5. How will you monitor and determine if the personalized principal support met expectations? How will you assess the effectiveness of all principal support programs?

## REFERENCES

Arnold, R. D., & Wade, J. P. (2015). A definition of systems thinking: A systems approach. *Procedia Computer Science, 44,* 669–678.

Bottoms, G., & Schmidt-Davis, J. (2010, August). *The three essentials: Improving schools requires district vision, district and state support, and principal leadership, 27.* The Wallace Foundation.

Covey, S. R. (1993). *First things first.* Simon & Schuster.

Farver, A. R., & Holt, C. R. (2015). Value of coaching in building leadership capacity of principals in urban schools. *NCPEA Education Leadership Review of Doctoral Research, 2*(2). https://files.eric.ed.gov/fulltext/EJ1105730.pdf

Ford T., Lavigne A., Fiegener A., & Si S. (2020). Understand district support for leader development and success in the accountability era: A review of the literature using social-cognitive theories of motivation. *Review of Educational Research, 90*(2), 264–307. DOI: 10.3102/0034654319899723

Grissom, J. A., Egalite, A. J., & Lindsay, C. A. (2021). *How principals affect students and schools: A systematic synthesis of two decades of research.* The Wallace Foundation.

Honig, M. I., & Rainey, L. R. (2014). Central office leadership in principal professional learning communities: The practice beneath the policy. *Teachers College Record, 116*(4), 1–48.

Hord, S. M. (2009a). Professional learning communities. *Journal of Staff Development, 30*(1), 40–43.

Iatarola, P., & Fruchter, N. (2004). District effectiveness: A study of investment strategies in New York City public schools and districts. *Educational Policy, 18*(3), 491–512.

National Institute of Excellence in Teaching. (2021). *The untapped potential of the principal supervisor.* https://www.niet.org/research-and-policy/show/policy/untapped-potential-principal-supervisor

Passmore, J. (2007). Coaching and mentoring—The role of experience and sector knowledge. *International Journal of Evidence Based Coaching and Mentoring,* 10–16.

Patterson, K., Grenny, J., McMillan, R., & Switzler, A. (2002). *Crucial conversations.* McGraw-Hill Contemporary.

Pelan, V. (2012, February). The difference between mentoring and coaching. *Talent Management Magazine.* https://people.themyersbriggs.com /rs/cpp/images/mentoring_and_coaching.pdf

Peterson, K. (2002). The professional development of principals: Innovations and opportunities. *Educational Administration Quarterly, 38*(2), 213–232.

Rogers, L. K., & VanGronigen, B. A. (2021). Beyond state approaches to early career principal induction. *Leadership and Policy in Schools, 1–25.*

Saphier, J., & Durkin, P. (2011). *Supervising principals: How superintendents can improve teaching and learning in the classroom.* https://www.ocmboces.org/tfiles/folder1608/Superintendents_supervising%20principals.pdf

Shoho, A. R., & Barnett, B. (2010). The realities of new principals: Challenges, joys, and sorrows. *Journal of School Leadership, 20*(5), 561–596.

Sinay, E. (2016). *Fostering a "culture of trust" within and outside a school system.* Toronto District School Board.

Sutcher, L., Podolsky, A., & Espinoza, D. (2017a). *Supporting principals' learning: Key features of effective programs.* Learning Policy Institute.

Tew, K. (2019, February). How a district prioritizes administrator PD. *Administration and Leadership.* https://www.edutopia.org/article/how-district-prioritizes-aministrator-pdf

Westberry, L. (2020). *Putting the pieces together: A systems approach to school leadership.* Rowman & Littlefield.

Wieczorek, D., & Manard, C. (2018). Instructional leadership challenges and practices of novice principals in rural schools. *Journal of Research in Rural Education, 34*(2), 1–21.

Wright, J., Siegrist, G., Pate, J., Monetti, D., & Raiford, S. (2009). Perceived induction needs for beginning principals. *International Journal of Educational Leadership Preparation, 4*(3), 1–13.

*Chapter 5*

# Principal Evaluation Practices That Support Individual and Organizational Growth

Kevin Badgett and Larry G. Daniel

Effective evaluation of employee performance starts with a mindset rather than a rubric, observation, or even a conversation (Heslin & Vande Walle, 2008; Mishra & Bost, 2018). When engaged as a formative process and focused on skill-building, employee performance evaluation offers many benefits. Those benefits include but are not limited to opportunities for growth, improvement in practice, and advancement for both individuals and organizations.

Evaluation can be poorly managed. When executed poorly or even in a clumsy manner, the performance evaluation process may only be an exercise in compliance at best. Used in an intentionally inappropriate or destructive way, evaluation can weaponize, disenfranchise, and poison organizational culture, not to mention what it can do to the employee who is the subject of the ill-intended evaluation.

The evaluation of principals is important because principal leadership and effectiveness matter. DeMatthews et al. (2020) asserted that principals are engaged in a broad range of leadership and management tasks. These include but are not limited to employee recruitment and retention, the shaping of culture, setting of organizational priorities, and providing resources.

Principals can also be thought of as policy "quarterbacks" and are responsible for leadership in everything related to instruction among many other responsibilities. Because the evaluation process has the potential to offer a vehicle to support reflection and improvement, failure to establish and execute it effectively can limit a principal's opportunities for growth and reflection and, by extension, a school community's ability to experience improvement in teaching and learning.

It is also important to acknowledge that principal performance does not happen in a vacuum. "Cookie-cutter" evaluations and evaluation processes have limited value for advancing a principal's growth and improvement in their practice (DeMatthews et al., 2020). Principal evaluations must be grounded in the standards for professional practice, and these evaluation practices must reside in evidence-based support. Such an approach acknowledges the centrality of professional standards while it also accommodates for applying a process to bring about specific and individually relevant growth goals.

What follows is an exploration of the practice of principal evaluation as a purposefully structured process intended to support shared efforts between principals and the district leaders who evaluate a principal's effectiveness. This chapter will link principal evaluation to its place in a process that includes support and ground principal evaluation as a formative and developmental process, not a purely summative one. This chapter furthermore presents principal evaluation as a collaborative endeavor that fosters skill-building in a way that contributes to the principal's ability to lead the school to greater levels of success.

In order to explore this topic in a systematic way, the authors will layer in the following dimensions and considerations for practitioners and preparation programs:

- The importance of a growth mindset to the process of performance evaluation
- Evaluation as an experience
- The importance of evaluation
- Elements of an effective evaluation
- Connectedness between principal growth and campus advancement
- Formative versus Summative Process
- General recap and framework considerations for the evaluation process
- Scenarios and discussion points for clinical exploration

## THE IMPORTANCE OF A GROWTH MINDSET TO THE PROCESS OF PERFORMANCE EVALUATION

It is important to acknowledge that the evaluator's mindset in the execution of an evaluation and appraisal process matters because the evaluator brings a "lens" to the appraisal process. Mishra and Bost (2018) illustrated how a preset lens can influence appraisals in their findings that raters' judgment of performance is informed by how they value independence and interdependence along a continuum.

According to their findings, supervisors who value independence place less weight on cooperative behaviors that they characterize as citizenship-related and more weight (in impact on evaluation) on what the authors deemed were "counterproductive performance behaviors" (p. 850). Citizenship behaviors are said to relate to an organization's goals but not to necessarily add to an organization's core functioning. Counterproductive behaviors are said to be those that impede goal accomplishment for an organization and can include but are not necessarily limited to theft or substance abuse.

Heslin and VandeWalle (2008) found that mindsets related to perceptions of the nature of behaviors as fixed or malleable also inform an evaluator's appraisal of an employee. These authors found that when an evaluator believes behaviors are malleable, he or she is more likely to perceive and acknowledge changes in behavior (specifically related to improvement) than would an evaluator who leans toward a mindset that views behaviors as fixed. Heslin and VandeWalle's grounded assertion then is that effective managers bring a mindset that looks for distinct behavioral changes (for good or bad) and allows related findings to inform the process.

This idea of mindset becomes important in the context of an appraisal when one considers how mindset informs preparation for and execution of an appraisal process for principals—specifically around equipping and fostering growth for improving the effectiveness of the principal being evaluated. When the principal appraiser begins with a focus and approach that emphasizes skill-building and support for growth rather than as an approach to deficit finding and/or compliance, the appraiser is more likely to start the evaluation process with the goal of fostering growth.

Beginning with the specific end of professional growth in mind, the principal appraiser, usually someone who has been in a comparable role, should be sensitive to the reality that principals are responsible for the overall operation of the campus. This has implications related to the systemic nature of organizational function (i.e., management of the various mechanical aspects of school leadership while also addressing leadership in instruction, visioning, and culture building). The effective evaluator is, therefore, prepared ahead of time with a belief that the principal can improve—at least until that evaluator has objective evidence to the contrary.

Although campus leadership is centrally focused on the principal's role as the chief instructional leader, consideration must be given to safety and operational effectiveness of the physical plant, management of systems and processes like the cafeteria, custodial and maintenance needs, a public relations face for the campus, human resources management, and many more facets and tasks. As such, the effective principal evaluator is always looking for ways to grow the principal as an effective coordinator of resources (e.g., time, materials, finances, technology, people, etc.) and systemic capacity builder (e.g., in students, teachers, parents).

## EVALUATION AS AN EXPERIENCE

It is often said that "perception is reality." This cliché statement communicates that an individual's perception defines his/her truth. This cliché has many problems when considered objectively. However, although perception is objectively *not* reality, it is true that perceptions have real consequences. The way an individual feels about a thing will most certainly impact how that individual interfaces with that thing, irrespective of the degree to which the individual's perception is factually accurate.

For that reason, it is important for district leaders to work with their campus leadership to co-construct meaning around what "we" will value and what will drive "our" decision-making as it relates to goals and the evaluation of goal accomplishment—this most certainly includes how principals are evaluated and how sense is made out of the evaluation process. This process of co-construction is important in part because such an approach invites investment into the work of making meaning and, as a by-product, fosters an environment of shared accountability.

With that framework in place as a lens, there is also some value in establishing something in the way of operational values to support the forthcoming discussion about the execution of an evaluation process that will be considered valid and that will effectively foster improvement of practice and, by extension, greater levels of student learning. Some of those definitions include but are not limited to the importance of the evaluation, elements of an effective evaluation, connectedness between principal growth and campus success, and a recognition of the formative nature of principal evaluation.

## THE IMPORTANCE OF EVALUATION

A general exploration of principal evaluation prompts the questions "why evaluate" and "what makes an evaluation effective." In responding to these questions, there is some value in recognizing that evaluation of employee work and effectiveness happens across industries. Consistently, organizations appreciate the value of the idea that "what gets measured is what gets done."

So, why do we evaluate? According to the performance evaluation handbook for the city of Flagstaff, Arizona (n.d.), formal evaluation of an employee's work performance offers baseline data that supports the employee's ability to build on identified strengths and to improve efficiency and effectiveness in areas where growth is needed. Similarly, the Texas Education Agency (2020) asserted that evaluation of principals is important to inform improvement for principals, guide principals' reflection about their practice to foster improvement, inform professional development efforts and programs, and improve principal leadership.

In a more expansive look at principal evaluation approaches across the country, Fuller et al. (2015) found multiple and diverse statements of purpose for principal evaluation. The stated purposes were related to direct and indirect impact on campus operation and success and included identifying needed professional development efforts for a principal, a focus on improving student learning outcomes, offering formative feedback to the evaluated leader, improving teacher performance around instruction, identifying effective leaders, and grounding personnel-related decisions (e.g., retention, compensation).

It is particularly interesting to note that evaluation as a process that supports personnel-related decisions was noted by these authors at the end of their list of findings. Although that does not mean personnel-related decision-making is unimportant, it seems it may not be the most important function of the evaluation process. This merits an exploration of elements of an effective evaluation.

## Elements of an Effective Evaluation

Having established some of the reasons for evaluation, what makes the evaluation effective and why should that matter? According to Fuller et al. (2015), there has historically been an inconsistent and uncoordinated approach to principal evaluation at the national level and an accompanying lack of confidence related to the quality or usefulness of those evaluation instruments. This is concerning in that it is difficult to earn buy-in from principals if they have little to no confidence in the evaluation process or the instruments being used.

A study on a relatively new principal appraisal instrument in Texas, T-PESS, identified some characteristics of a principal evaluation process said to be effective and beneficial by principals who were appraised with that instrument. According to DeMatthews et al., those characteristics included being "'less-punitive,' 'more focused,' 'efficient,' 'growth-minded,' and 'more aligned' to the principal's job" (p. 13). Other aspects of the process noted as important included reflection, opportunities to self-assess, participation in goal-setting, and the value of the scoring rubric that serves as the lens for the evaluation process.

What emerges here is a picture that evaluation is valued and considered effective when it is objective, actionable for the individual being evaluated, and engaged as a process in a collaborative manner. Although it is true that evaluations can and should inform personnel decisions (as previously indicated), when used effectively, evaluations are far more about building capacity for leadership in a way that supports the teaching and learning objectives for the campus community the principal leads than they are about only justifying personnel-related action or simply engaging in an exercise in compliance.

## Connectedness—Principal Growth and Campus Advancement

Differentiation is an important principle when preparing for an appraisal process. No two principals are alike and although the appraiser's experience can be deeply instructive, that experience, no matter how ranged or diverse, will rarely ever offer a summarily comprehensive "story" or lesson set for a principal being evaluated. For that reason, it is important that the evaluator cultivate an ability to diagnose needs for each principal they serve and responsively adjust accordingly. That being acknowledged, the principal is not the only diverse "player" in the scenario.

It may seem obvious, but in a compliance-driven setting informed by state and federal programmatic and operational requirements, it is sometimes easy to overlook the fact that no one campus is like another. Although this may seem to be obvious, it is important to consider the implications for the evaluation process. Such implications are expansive; a failure to explore them could complicate the efficacy of the evaluation process.

As previously explored, principals are leading complex, multidimensional organizations where decisions are never made in a vacuum and each decision made will have a systemic impact on multiple facets of the campus operation. The effective principal evaluator is prepared to approach the appraisal process with data that informs him or her of the make-up of a campus. This includes being aware of local needs and factors borne out by research to contribute to success in teaching and learning.

Local needs and campus culture can differ widely from one setting to another—even within a single district. As such, it is important that the principal evaluator *know* the campus and the dynamics at play on that campus. Conversations with school leadership, teachers, students, parents, and others in the community can help calibrate the evaluator's diagnostic lens in a way that will support their ability to determine the degree to which the principal is sensitive to the context in which they are operating. The evaluator can then strategically plan their approach to helping that principal plan to address relevant needs through the appraisal process.

Research has also offered insight into general factors to contribute to or impede success in advancing student mastery and characteristics of students served on a campus should be considered when determining principal effectiveness (Fuller et al., 2015). Although not exhaustive, some of those factors include student behavior (US Department of Education, 2010), a student's sociocultural context (Thomson, 2018), the economic status of students and their families (Bozkurt et al., 2021) and, of course, the teacher, which is why efforts around retention are so important (Rosenblatt et al., 2019).

At the intersection of these various applications for differentiation, the principal evaluator has an opportunity to use a process that should be about fostering growth to positively invest in both the principal and in the campus the principal leads. Although much about a standardized principal evaluation process should be connected to standards and transferable skills, the application of the process happens in a specific time and place and not in theoretical space.

Equipped with contextually sensitive data, the effective evaluator does not stop at applying an appraisal process to its primary function, skill-building and support for the principal being evaluated. Rather, a process applied in a real school setting also cultivates a greater sensitivity to the data-informed needs of students on the campus. Executed well, the principal evaluator becomes more than a technician completing an exercise in compliance. Rather, that person becomes a strategic support resource who contributes to advancing teaching and learning by helping the principal refine their practice to meet needs in the "real world" on their campus.

## Formative versus Summative Process

The technician's approach to evaluation engages the appraisal process as a summative one that is completed as a function of compliance and form. Success and growth are a secondary consideration at best. In doing so, this person checks the box, completes the task, and meets threshold job requirements. That person likely operates in a system that values management. Unfortunately, where processes can be managed, people need to be led.

Leading effectively requires a situational awareness or being sensitive to what Parse (2018) called a "now-moment." This filter requires a formative approach characterized by partnership between the principal and the evaluator and situates the appraisal process as one that is an ongoing support relationship. Conceptually framed in this way, the evaluator better diagnoses the needs of the moment, perceives those needs across time, offers a more accurate appraisal, and, most importantly, better supports teaching and learning on the campus where that principal serves.

## General Recap and Framework Considerations for the Evaluation Process

In this summarized section of the chapter, the reader will find an outline-based approach recapping salient points and offering something of a framework; however, it is important to avoid mechanical and/or technically prescriptive processes. The reader should appreciate this is less about prescriptive mechanics and more about principles of support and possible ways of application. Such an understanding reinforces the importance of operating out of a deep sensitivity to the context and the importance of skill-building and support which, as a by-product, also meets compliance requirements—rather than being compliance-driven.

### The Mindset

An understanding of the evaluation process begins with the understanding of the mindset and intent of the evaluator. This implies the evaluator is engaged as a reflective practitioner and *partner* with the principal in the appraisal process. Such an approach is vital to a successful evaluation process that builds capacity in the principal and equips the principal with insight and skills needed to advance teaching and learning on the campus. As previously illustrated, evaluation of principals is important, but it is at least as important that the process be executed by beginning with the proper mindset.

### Evaluation to a Purpose and with a Co-constructed Meaning

The authors concede that not everyone in a given principal role is right for that role or, sometimes, for the principalship at all. However, most principals are appointed for a reason and there is reason to have confidence in their competence and professionalism. For that reason alone (and there are certainly others that could be explored), it seems reasonable to start with the expectation that the principal is insightful, intelligent, and a worthy partner in the appraisal process.

Starting with an articulation of shared goals and co-constructed meaning sets the framework for a shared effort based on shared values and a calibrated lens around what "we" will value during the appraisal process. In addition to generating enthusiasm together, this kind of approach just makes sense and, executed well and with good faith, can make the process more enjoyable and successful and lead to less headache for both parties.

### Characteristics of an Effective Evaluation

What is "best" for each appraisal will depend on contextual factors previously explored. For that reason, it is important not to overgeneralize. Avoiding the temptation to overgeneralize, however, is not the same thing as failing to develop a playbook of helpful approaches. Said another way, principal appraisers can most certainly engage the process with confidence knowing that there are some things that make the appraisal work well.

Research has demonstrated appraisals are more effective when they are focused, efficient, targeted to growth, and clearly aligned to the principal's job responsibilities. Principals perceive value in the process when it includes opportunities for reflection, self-evaluation, and opportunities to participate in goal-setting. Finally, some type of standardized, objective scoring rubric that informs evaluation and serves as a tool against which to calibrate shared expectations can offer quality assurance and lend credence to an end-of-year appraisal report.

## Advancement of Teaching and Learning

Principal evaluation has several functions and purposes, but, ultimately, everything educators do is about advancing teaching and learning. Principal evaluation is no exception. It is an opportunity for the evaluator to collaborate with the principal in an exploration of ways to improve the principal's skills so that teachers are more effectively supported and so that student mastery of content improves. Principal leadership matters as it applies to student learning. The evaluator should work with the principal to ensure a purposeful by-product of their efforts is a positive impact on teaching and learning across the campus.

## Formative, Not Summative

Finally, effective principal evaluation is a formative process and not a summative one. A summative approach to evaluation is grounded in compliance. To be clear, compliance is important. There is a reason for most of the rules that govern school operations; however, adherence to compliance can become dogmatic, and the rationale for the rule can be lost. For that reason, balance between the what (evaluation) and the why (growth and support) must be established.

Managed well, compliance in the execution of the evaluation process can be positive and make positive contributions to student learning. To do that, however, evaluation must be formative. This means frequent meetings throughout the period of an appraisal that is evidence-informed and targeted to meet data-informed needs. Because the appraisal process involves people, those needs evolve and change throughout the year. A formative process supports the ability of both parties to make adjustments and accommodations as appropriate over time.

## SUMMARY

What gets measured gets done. There is little doubt that measuring the right things as part of a proper process can support the district's ability to hold campus leadership accountable for student outcomes; however, accountability starts with the evaluator. Before pronouncing a summative judgment of a principal's effectiveness as a leader on that campus, the evaluator should take a look inside and consider how effectively they have filled their role as a resourcer and capacity builder. That is the first step and is connected to the idea of starting with a right mindset.

At the end of an evaluation process, it is important to note that although not everything that happens on a campus is a principal's fault, everything that happens on a campus is a principal's responsibility. Somewhere in the space between those thoughts one can find how accountability paired with meaningful support can inform a principal evaluation process that equips the principal and advances teaching and learning on the campus that the principal leads.

## SCENARIOS FOR CLINICAL PREPARATION

The authors hope this chapter's contents will be instructive to district leaders who currently support principals as evaluators by offering a chance to reflect on their own practices. Such reflection may highlight opportunities to refine practice and mindfulness that improvement comes over time. For that reason, it may be the best place to start in improving practice is to make an adjustment or refinement in one area that has been explored.

Growth in practice continues and compounds by moving to another area to refine after the first area is refined appropriately. Over time, that kind of approach will build a solid toolkit to support the evaluator's approach to the appraisal process and support their efforts to mentor future district leaders who will one day evaluate principals. This idea is grounded in the reality that continuous improvement happens over time, not overnight.

The authors also hope the content of this chapter will be helpful to support clinical preparation for aspirant district leaders who will be serving as principal evaluators in the future. For that reason, two different scenarios are included to support clinical discussions in a low-risk environment. In other words, these scenarios will offer candidates in district leadership preparation programs an opportunity to practice decision-making without having to experience the consequences of those decisions.

The scenarios are hypothetical circumstances and not informed by actual real-world cases. Any perceived similarities between these cases and actual experiences are therefore purely coincidental.

## SCENARIO 1

### The New Principal

Esther Gomez has recently been appointed to lead Walter Smith Elementary as the new principal. After having spent three years as an assistant principal in a neighboring district, this is Esther's first appointment as a lead principal. In addition to her leadership experience, Ms. Gomez previously served as a teacher at the first, third, and fourth grade levels and for two years as a teacher leader who provided general instructional and management support and direction for teachers.

Esther's primary focus in her previous role was support of teachers who taught in grade levels where students were administered the state's high-stakes exam. She was appointed because of the superintendent's confidence in her instructional leadership, particularly in the area of math, and in the confidence she projects as a leader. Esther has a strong command of state curriculum expectations and a record of effectiveness as a teacher and school leader.

The campus where Gomez previously served as an assistant principal had a record of academic success, was situated in a relatively affluent area of a neighboring district, and hosted a student population that comprised 25 percent low socioeconomic status. Ten percent of the students were English language learners, and 7 percent of the students were served with special education resources and support.

The student body on the campus was racially and ethnically diverse. Approximately 50 percent of the student body were of Hispanic descent, 30 percent were white, 10 percent were African American, and 5 percent were Asian. The remaining groups of students were split between Pacific Islander and Two or More Races. This campus enjoyed a low faculty/staff turnover rate and leadership from a lead principal in the position for the last seven years who succeeded a principal who stayed in that position for twelve years. This campus enjoyed the support of a stable parent organization and broad parent support.

Smith Elementary is a school in need of assistance. With a record of academic failure for the last three years and inconsistent leadership for the last five, Smith needs a clear vision and a steady hand in leadership. Ms. Gomez will be the fourth principal in the last five years and inherits a faculty and staff that has seen 25 percent turnover in the last year and 50 percent turnover in the last four years. A look at the demographic make-up of the school reveals a campus that is very different from the campus where Esther served as an assistant principal for three years.

A sharp contrast, Smith Elementary hosts a student population that comprised 73 percent low socioeconomic status. Thirty-two percent of the students were English language learners and 14 percent of the students were served with special education resources and support. The differentiated learning needs for this campus will be different when compared with Esther's experience. She will need to have a plan.

The student body at Smith is also racially and ethnically diverse. Approximately 62 percent of the student body were of Hispanic descent, 17 percent were white, 15 percent were African American, and 2 percent were Asian. The remaining groups of students were split between Pacific Islander and Two or More Races. There is little in the way of active or meaningful support from parents at Smith Elementary. Parent interactions with faculty and staff can typically be described as passing and usually only during pickup, dismissal, or when disciplinary actions are necessary.

## The Principal Appraiser

As Esther's evaluator this year, you share the superintendent's enthusiasm about her appointment. You have had multiple opportunities to interact with Esther and, during the interview process, you were given the opportunity to share your perspective about her potential hire. As a member of the district-level leadership team for the last two years, you have some knowledge of Smith Elementary and its challenges.

Having been a new principal who led a successful turnaround effort in a challenging school yourself, you also have a measure of empathy for the challenge ahead for Ms. Gomez. Consistently, despite your confidence in Esther's capacity, you have to develop a plan to ensure you are offering the support and insight she will need as she begins her first year in service as the principal of Walter Smith Elementary.

## Important Considerations

Because you realize an effective appraisal process is something that is completed over time and not a report informed by a moment in time, you are sensitive to the need to conduct research, gather data, engage in conversations, and build relationships. As you begin this process, there are a number of important considerations that will inform early efforts. While not exhaustive, some of the important considerations are found below. Please take time to build a plan for your approach to completing a robust and well-supported appraisal of Esther Gomez during her first year as the lead principal at Smith Elementary.

- How will you prepare for the evaluation process in a way that ensures you bring a proper mindset to your work?

- How will you help ensure Ms. Gomez has a strong start?
  - How will you help her anticipate the differences between needs at her former campus and this one?
  - What systems access will she have?
  - What systems will be similar to your district as compared with the one she left?
  - How will you ensure she is oriented to your district's culture, climate, and norms?
  - With whom should Ms. Gomez network? Is there an experienced principal in the district who can serve as a nonevaluating mentor/support resource?
- What is your plan for presence and formative discussions?
  - How will you orient Ms. Gomez to the evaluation instrument/process for your district?
  - How will you engage this new principal in conversations about areas for her professional development?
  - What resources does the district have or is the district willing to fund to support her growth as a new principal?
  - How often will you meet with Ms. Gomez?
  - What diagnostic tools/resources do you have at your disposal to support her formative exploration of her new role?
- How will you collect data to inform the evaluation process?
  - What data disaggregation and aggregation tools/software will you use?
  - How will you orient Ms. Gomez to these to ensure she is a partner in discussions during which you can make meaning out of the data?
  - With whom will you visit to learn about campus operations and about how Ms. Gomez's leadership is impacting those operations?
  - What observations will you make?
    - What do you see in students?
    - What do you see in parents?
    - What do you see in teachers?
  - How will your findings inform/support formative conversations with Ms. Gomez?
  - How will you use data to help Ms. Gomez connect her leadership to student learning outcomes?
- How will you determine which leadership style to use when supporting Ms. Gomez?
  - What behaviors might you look for in how Ms. Gomez leads to make a determination about your approach?
  - What behaviors might you look for in how Ms. Gomez responds to you to make a determination about a best approach?
- How do you plan to pace your observations?

○ Will you meet once a month, twice a month, or once a quarter?
  ○ How will Ms. Gomez's schedule and need inform your plan?

Be mindful that a plan can change and likely should as you gather additional data. However, you will want to plan. Failure to do so will likely undermine your efforts.

These considerations are not exhaustive but will offer the aspiring and/or novice district-level leader a number of starting points for reflection and planning. Discussion leaders (e.g., professors or perhaps someone in a district-level position leading these discussions) may use these in a variety of settings that may include but would not necessarily be limited to individual narrative reflection/planning, small group discussion, discussion board interaction in an online setting, or as a resource to prompt planning for a possible real-world scenario.

## SCENARIO 2

### The New Principal Evaluator

You have just been appointed as the assistant superintendent in Toledo ISD and you cannot wait to begin! After having served in leadership positions on the campus for the last eight years with seven years as a teacher before that, you believe you bring experience and insight that will bring real value to the district community in Toledo. As the assistant superintendent, you will be responsible to conduct performance appraisals with each of the campus principals during the upcoming school year.

Having been on the other side of the process, you believe you bring an empathy to your role as a principal evaluator. However, while most of your experience was at the middle school level, you will also be responsible to complete appraisals with principals at six elementary campuses (PK–5), two middle school campuses (6–8), a comprehensive high school (10–12), and the district's disciplinary alternative education placement center (DAEP).

In anticipation of that task, you have asked for personnel files for and anecdotal information about each of the ten principals (there is a freshman center director who, as a high school associate principal, reports to the high school principal) you will supervise in the coming year. You understand that getting to know the people you will be leading will not be complete by reviewing files and hearing from the superintendent, but collecting these data will offer some context as you begin preparation for the evaluation process. The bulleted points below represent initial summary findings:

- Two of the elementary principals are brand-new principals. One served in the district as an assistant principal for four years before his promotion.

One served as an assistant principal out of district for three years before her appointment to the lead principal role this year.
- Two of the elementary principals are established in the district for at least ten years and have a record of steady success.
- One of the elementary principals has served as the principal at that campus for twenty-five years with varying degrees of success over time. Student performance on standardized exams in the past three years has trended downward. The trends are not stark but they are consistent. This principal was serving in that role before you started your career as an educator and was on that campus for twenty years when the superintendent was appointed.
- The last of the elementary principals has just completed her first year in the role. The superintendent has shared she believes in the principal and her capacity, but there was a concerning amount of turnover on that campus from the last year to this one.
- One of the middle school principals was just placed at that school after years of success as the principal at one of the district elementary schools. While she is new to this campus as a principal, she has eight years of experience as an elementary principal.
- The second middle school principal has been serving in that role for the last six years. You've learned that he applied for the job you now have. He is respected, well-liked, and has been successful in his role.
- The high school principal is a district native. He attended school as a student in Toledo and worked his way into the principalship by starting as a teacher/coach, moving into an assistant principal role, then to associate, and then to principal. His leadership approach is direct. He is respected as a strong manager but started in the role in a time when instructional leadership was given less emphasis. Students have always done well enough, but the culture of the school emphasizes athletics and is said to have a "good old boy" system.
- Finally, the principal at the DAEP has served at this school for four years. This past year was her second as principal after having served for two years as the assistant principal. This principal has announced her retirement at the end of the current academic year.

Having reviewed files and gathered this information, what are your most important next steps?

While not exhaustive, some of the considerations that may be important as you start this work include the following:

- How will you begin the appraisal process?
- What questions will you ask?

- How does what you know about the principals inform your approach plan?
- What additional data are available to support your preparation and review?
- How will you diagnose campus-level needs and use what you learn to inform your approach to supporting each principal?
- How will you plan for differentiation?
- What training might benefit you as a new principal evaluator?

As you begin your preparation, it will be important to be mindful of a few things:

- You have the superintendent's confidence and bring remarkable experience and insight. You would not have been appointed over the internal candidate if that were not the case.
- Despite having great experience, you will need to differentiate your approach and an application of the appraisal process in a way that is best suited to meet the needs of each principal and the school community they lead while applying the appraisal rubric with fidelity.
- Each principal is ultimately responsible for the campus community he/she leads; however, you are responsible for the tone you set in the appraisal process. A successful evaluation starts with you.
  - How will you determine the best approach?
  - What standard questions might be appropriate for all principals?
  - What "clues" from your analysis may inform a need for differentiation?
- How will you go about a process that will give you insight into the campus community each principal leads?
- How will what you learn inform your approach to evaluation and support for each principal?

As with the first scenario, these considerations are not exhaustive but will offer the aspiring and/or novice district-level leader a number of starting points for reflection and planning. The authors recommend that discussion leaders (e.g., professors or perhaps someone in a district-level position leading these discussions) use these in a variety of settings that may include but would not necessarily be limited to individual narrative reflection/planning, small group discussion, discussion board interaction in an online setting, or as a resource to prompt planning for a possible real-world scenario.

## REFERENCES

Bozkurt, S., Çoban, Ö., Özdemir, M., & Özdemir, N. (2021). How leadership, school culture, collective efficacy, academic self-efficacy, and socioeconomic status affect student achievement. *Egitimve Bilim, 46*(207).

City of Flagstaff, A. Z. (n.d.). *Performance evaluation guidelines*. https://www.flagstaff.az.gov/DocumentCenter/View/9869/Performance-Evaluation-Handbook?bidId=

DeMatthews, D. E., Scheffer, M., & Kotok, S. (2021). Useful or useless? Principal perceptions of the Texas principal evaluation and support system. *Journal of Research on Leadership Education, 16*(4), 279–304. DOI: 10.1177/1942775120933920

Fuller, E. J., Hollingworth, L., & Liu, J. (2015). Evaluating state principal evaluation plans across the United States. *Journal of Research on Leadership Education, 10*(3), 164–192.

Heslin, P. A., & VandeWalle, D. (2008). Managers' implicit assumptions about personnel. *Current Directions in Psychological Science, 17*(3), 219–223.

Keigher, A. (2010). *Teacher attrition and mobility: Results from the 2008–09 teacher follow-up survey. First look*. NCES 2010-353. National Center for Education Statistics.

Mishra, V., & Bost, M., Jr. (2018). Investigating the effects of cultural-mindset priming on evaluation of job performance behaviors. *Europe's Journal of Psychology, 14*(4), 846.

Parse, R. R. (2018). Situational awareness: A leadership phenomenon. *Nursing Science Quarterly, 31*(4), 317–318.

Rosenblatt, K., Badgett, K., & Eldridge, J. (2019). Teacher retention: Important considerations for rural and urban districts in Texas. *International Journal of Innovative Business Strategies, 5*(1), 274–278.

Texas Principal Evaluation and Support System. (2020, June 26). *May a district use the T-PESS evaluation system for an assistant principal (FAQ)*. https://tpess.org/faq/

Thomson, S. (2018). Achievement at school and socioeconomic background – An educational perspective. *NPJ Science of Learning, 3*(1), 1–2. DOI: 10.1038/s41539-018-0022-0

*Chapter 6*

# Setting the Destination and Charting the Course

## *Higher-Education Opportunities for K–12 Leaders Engaged in Systems Improvement*

Noelle Paufler

### INTRODUCTION

Leaders of K–12 schools and districts lead complex organizations. These organizations are systems with their own support structures and processes (Westberry, 2020). As a K–12 leader, it is important to understand what structures are needed, how to put those in place, and how to sustain them over time (Westberry, 2020). Leaders also need to know how to engage with stakeholders to effectively implement change within the system. Educational leaders seeking opportunities to deepen their own understanding of educational systems and further develop their knowledge and skills are better prepared to serve their school communities.

Effectively leading a complex organization requires a growth mindset. Individuals with a growth mindset continuously seek opportunities for professional learning. Such leaders believe their basic personal qualities can be cultivated through their own efforts and strategies and with help from others (Dweck, 2006). This mindset is reflected in a lifelong passion for learning, based on a belief that "a person's true potential is unknown (and unknowable); that it's impossible to foresee what can accomplished with years of passion, toil, and training" (Dweck, 2006, p. 7). Thus, the professional growth of the leader supports growth in the organization.

Higher-education institutions offer K–12 school and district leaders a variety of opportunities for ongoing professional learning, both formal and informal. Engaging in ongoing professional learning either through advanced degrees or collaborative university school-district partnerships can further develop in leaders the knowledge and skills they need to effectively implement change. These opportunities for learning and engagement can foster professional growth and support career advancement.

Understanding the various opportunities available through higher-education institutions that support professional development is an important first step for educational leaders. There are myriad considerations for leaders as they determine which opportunities will help them develop professionally and advance in their careers. Understanding the personal and professional commitments required to pursue higher-education opportunities is critical for success.

## SETTING THE DESTINATION

### Opportunities for Advanced Study Supporting Leadership Development

Higher-education institutions offer programs for advanced study that can help educational leaders develop the knowledge and skills needed to be effective in their leadership roles (Young, 2006). Leaders who possess a broad knowledge base and deep understanding of educational systems, how they operate, who is involved, and the ways they shape local practice are better equipped to lead continuous improvement efforts in their district or school.

Leaders with a keen awareness of how systems-level factors influence teachers and students at the school level know how to ask critical questions about what needs to change and how to engage others in the process (Hinnant-Crawford, 2020). Efforts to lead systems improvement are enhanced when leaders seek formal educational opportunities to develop their knowledge of improvement principles and skills in applying research-based practices (Bryk et al., 2015). A variety of advanced (graduate-level) certificates, credentials, and degree programs offer such opportunities for leadership development.

The nomenclature for and availability of such opportunities for advanced study in the field of education vary across the United States. These offerings are influenced by various state and national requirements (e.g., state approval of programs for professional certification/licensure and national accreditation for higher-education institutions).

Classroom teachers interested in administration can earn a master's degree (e.g., Master of Education or MEd in educational administration or leadership) and obtain their state school-/building-level administrator certificate or license. Teachers who already have a master's degree in teaching or their subject area may obtain their administrator certificate or license by completing a postbaccalaureate or graduate certificate. Administrators seeking opportunities beyond a master's degree might pursue micro-credentials or advanced degree programs such as the Education Specialist (EdS), Doctor of Education (EdD), and Doctor of Philosophy (PhD).

*Micro-Credentials*

Micro-credentials offer personalized professional development for educators seeking to demonstrate skill mastery in specific areas. With their focus on personalization, competency, flexibility, cost efficiency, and collaboration, micro-credentials reflect a departure from traditional professional development (Hunt et al., 2020; Woods & Woods, 2021). Although once less common in education, educators now have many options available to develop their skills through relevant content delivered in flexible modalities (Hunt et al., 2020; Woods & Woods, 2021).

Micro-credentials are currently included in nine states' Every Student Succeeds Act plans as a way for educators to earn continuing education credits (Hunt et al., 2020). They can be completed informally (noncredit-bearing) or formally (credit-bearing) in a relatively short period of time. Educators' micro-credentials can be certified by private organizations or higher-education institutions.

Educators can complete micro-credentials independently by earning digital badges via private virtual learning platforms (Greene, 2019). These digital badges certify specific skills and become part of a personal digital profile. For example, Digital Promise, originally authorized by Congress as the National Center for Research in Advanced Information and Digital Technologies, has been offering micro-credentials since 2008. Digital Promise also serves as a platform for other organizations, of which there are currently more than fifty (e.g., Center for Teaching Quality, Facebook, National Geographic Society), offering their own micro-credentials.

Higher-education institutions also offer micro-credentials as a cost-effective learning experience for educators seeking to develop skills but not earn a degree (Rottman & Duggan, 2021). For example, educators can demonstrate leadership competencies in topic areas such as human capital management, school operations, equity and cultural responsiveness, and community engagement as part of a certificate or advanced degree program. Whether completed independently or through a higher-education program, micro-credentials offer educators expanded opportunities to broaden their knowledge base and develop leadership skills.

*Advanced Degree Programs*

**Education Specialist.** The EdS is a graduate-level degree that prepares practitioners for an advanced career in the field of education. The EdS typically requires a similar number of credits as a master's degree and can be completed in two to three years. However, the coursework offers greater depth in a specialization area (e.g., educational administration or leadership, curriculum, instructional technology, and counseling). In this regard, the EdS provides an opportunity for advanced preparation between a master's and doctorate.

EdS programs are designed for educators who are already working full-time in educational settings. These include, for example, school-level administrators who would like to qualify for other leadership positions. During the 2017–2018 school year, 25.9 percent of principals in K–12 public schools had an EdS degree (US Department of Education, National Center for Education Statistics [NCES], 2019).

Obtaining the EdS can help educators develop professionally in a variety of ways, including advancing into a leadership role, improving in the field, and transitioning into another area of teaching. Since the EdS is intended for educators who already have a bachelor's and master's degree, principals with a master's degree in educational administration or leadership could pursue the EdS to be competitive for leadership opportunities at the district level.

The EdS can help educators seeking advanced mastery in their current area of specialization. For example, completing graduate-level coursework in administration or leadership as an EdS specialization area can help principals improve their leadership skills and increase their effectiveness in their current role. Earning the EdS can also help educators seeking to transition into another area of teaching. Principals with a teaching certificate or license in a subject area who would like to return to the classroom could use the EdS to transition into another teaching role (e.g., special education and career and technical education).

While the EdS can help classroom teachers develop mastery in their subject area and instructional pedagogy, most educators pursue this degree to qualify for a leadership role outside of the classroom. Pursuing the EdS with a specialization area can help principals qualify for positions at the district level. Specialization areas offered as part of the EdS often include administration or leadership, counseling, curriculum design, instructional technology, and reading and literacy, among others.

EdS programs may also offer specializations in early childhood, elementary, secondary, and special education; however, these are not usually intended to prepare graduates for certification or licensure as a classroom teacher. EdS programs can lead to other endorsements, depending upon state certification or licensure requirements. Completing the EdS can also serve as preparation for doctoral-level study.

**Doctor of Education.** There are two doctoral degrees available in the field of education, the EdD and PhD. During the 2017–2018 school year, 10.5 percent of principals in K–12 public schools had a doctorate (US Department of Education, NCES, 2019). Both degrees generally require a minimum of fifty credits beyond the master's degree and can be completed in three to four years, although the specific number of credits required and length of time to completion vary based on program/institutional requirements and student-specific goals and needs.

There are distinct differences, however, between the EdD and PhD in terms of their career and degree objectives, although these are more clearly distinguishable at some institutions than others. The EdD is typically considered an applied professional doctorate for educators currently working in the field. In contrast, the PhD is typically more research-based and intended to prepare educators for research and teaching roles in higher education and other educational agencies.

The EdD can help educators develop as leaders in several ways, such as broadening their knowledge and skills, enhancing their competitiveness for advanced leadership positions, and preparing them to solve complex, systemic problems in the field. The EdD is intended to provide practitioners with the theoretical and practical knowledge and research skills needed for leadership roles in a variety of settings. Such settings include K–12 school districts, government agencies, and public and private organizations providing educational or related services.

A strong scholarly background and ability to apply their learning in practice enhances EdD graduates' competitiveness for advanced leadership positions. EdD students often complete the state requirements for certification or licensure as a district-level administrator as part of their program. Having the EdD helps principals applying for district-level leadership roles as superintendent, assistant superintendent, curriculum director, and so on, distinguish themselves from other candidates for those positions.

EdD programs focused on educational systems further prepare graduates to solve complex, persistent problems using a systems perspective. By pursuing the EdD, principals can develop both their scholarly knowledge base and understanding of how theory and research impact practice across K–12 education systems. They can then apply their learning to address problems in their schools (e.g., better support induction teachers, increase teacher retention, improve school climate) and ultimately improve student learning outcomes.

Although some EdD graduates become faculty at higher-education institutions, EdD programs are primarily focused on preparing graduates to lead educational organizations. Thus, ensuring graduates can apply their learning to practical situations is an important objective of the EdD. EdD students build a broad knowledge base in the areas of educational theory, research, and policy through relevant coursework and opportunities for field-based learning experiences.

EdD students demonstrate their understanding of research methods (i.e., study design, data collection, and analysis) by conducting applied research as part of course activities and their own dissertation study. As part of the EdD dissertation, often called a dissertation in practice, students apply theoretical and practical knowledge to design and conduct a research study to improve problem(s) in applied settings. EdD students often employ mixed-methods, action research, program evaluation, and other related designs for their dissertation.

Implications of the study findings for practice are among the most valued aspects of the EdD dissertation. Findings that demonstrate how to address complex, persistent problems at the systems level are useful for leaders beyond the research site. Educators who are interested in conducting research that is more theoretical than applied in nature might consider pursuing a PhD rather than an EdD.

**Doctor of Philosophy.** The PhD is a research-intensive doctorate intended to prepare researchers, scholars, and scholarly practitioners for roles in higher-education institutions (e.g., colleges and universities, community colleges), educational agencies (e.g., federal and state departments of education), and other organizations (e.g., research and policy centers/institutes, nonprofits).

While the PhD generally requires a minimum of fifty credits beyond the master's degree, the specific degree requirements and length of time to degree completion vary by program and institution. Some PhD students pursue their degree on a part-time basis while working in a full-time professional position. Others leave their employment to attend school as a full-time student, often holding part-time positions as graduate or research assistants in their department or college.

Obtaining the PhD can create new opportunities for career advancement, including as faculty conducting research and teaching in higher education, experts with extensive knowledge and skills in specific topic areas(s) or research method(s), and change agents informing policy and practice in the field. While principals who would like to teach in educator preparation programs (i.e., bachelor's, master's, EdS, and EdD) can have an EdD or PhD in educational administration, leadership, policy, or a related area, faculty who teach in research-intensive graduate-level programs generally have a PhD.

PhD programs help students develop expertise in one or more topic(s) or research method(s). Principals who want to become experts in, for example, educational policy or evaluation and assessment can choose one of these as a concentration area for their PhD. PhD graduates can utilize their expertise to inform research, policy, and practice in the field. Earning the PhD can help give credibility to principals who want to influence change beyond their school by engaging with legislators and policymakers on broader reform initiatives.

PhD students develop expertise while studying under the supervision of a faculty adviser/chair and committee of other faculty members. Students' coursework, field-based learning experiences, and dissertation are all intended to help them develop this expertise. In this regard, earning the PhD is personalized for each student. PhD students often develop and test theories on their topic as part of their dissertation and then continue to build upon their research (e.g., replication in other settings with new populations). Implications of the study findings for future research in addition to policy and practice are significant.

## Considerations for Leaders Pursuing an Advanced Degree

Advanced degree programs are generally intended to help graduates reach specific short- and long-term goals for growth and career advancement. There are many considerations for principals seeking opportunities for professional development in higher education. Obtaining information about the various advanced degree programs available is an important first step in the process.

Before selecting a degree program, it is helpful to learn about each program's requirements, objectives, curriculum, structure (e.g., cohort model, individualized), course format/modality (e.g., face-to-face, hybrid, online), and milestones (i.e., culminating activities such as the dissertation). Institutional membership in national, state, and regional consortia and professional organizations can also help shape program design and graduate learning objectives and outcomes. Learning about these aspects can help principals choose the right degree program to achieve their professional goals.

Understanding the personal and professional implications of pursuing an advanced degree is important for successful completion. Enrolling in graduate school requires a significant time commitment since most advanced degrees take two to four years to complete, depending upon whether students enroll on a full- or part-time basis. While courses can be offered in face-to-face, hybrid, and online (synchronous and asynchronous) formats, participating in and completing requirements for each course requires a sustained time commitment.

There is also a financial cost associated with pursuing an advanced degree. Since the cost of tuition, fees, materials, and so on, can vary significantly by program and institution, it is helpful to estimate the costs associated with each degree when selecting a program. In addition to time and financial commitments, students balance myriad personal and professional roles and responsibilities while pursuing their degree. For example, principals who enroll in an advanced degree program while working full time often grapple with how to fulfill their professional responsibilities as a school leader while completing coursework and other degree requirements.

In addition to selecting the right degree program and understanding the commitments necessary for completion, actively engaging in the learning process is critical for success. An advanced degree is intended to provide opportunities for professional growth that broaden students' knowledge base and enhance their skills in research and leadership. For principals, taking graduate courses in education can provide opportunities to critically read scholarly works, engage in dialogue with faculty and their peers, and apply their learning in the field.

Undertaking this process with an open mind and strong commitment to individual and collective growth enhances students' overall experience. In this way, obtaining an advanced degree helps foster leadership development and ideally leads to career advancement opportunities. Honing leadership skills furthers leaders' efforts to lead systemic change in their school community.

## CHARTING THE COURSE

### The Role of Collaborative Partnerships in Leadership for Change

In addition to the above opportunities for advanced study, K–12 leaders can also develop partnerships with higher-education faculty to support local change efforts. Such collaborative university-school district partnership offer another way to foster engagement between leaders in the field and university education faculty. These partnerships can help support leaders' professional growth and use of research to inform practice (Browne-Ferrigno & Sanzo, 2011).

Research-practice partnerships that promote reflective practices and ongoing engagement in the change process can be transformative for both K–12 leaders and faculty partners. Shared leadership and open communication between leaders and faculty can prompt successful change in local educational settings (Ralston et al., 2015). Engagement with K–12 leaders can also help faculty partners improve their university leadership preparation programs.

Effective partnerships offer myriad benefits for students, teachers, and educational leaders at the individual, school, and district levels. By engaging in collaborative partnerships, principals, for example, have greater opportunities to gain the knowledge and skills they need to effectively serve their school communities. Activities during which principals develop, practice, and receive feedback on leadership skills build confidence and foster communication among members of the partnership.

At the school level, increased access to resources and support from faculty can help principals implement initiatives that improve local conditions such as school climate (Kochan et al., 2021). In turn, by providing opportunities for principals' professional growth that promotes continuous school improvement efforts, partnerships also help districts build a leadership team prepared to address systemic challenges in innovative ways. In this regard, such partnerships can function as communities of practice (Wenger et al., 2002), within which K–12 leaders and university faculty learn from each other in formal and informal ways.

## A Model for Collaborative Partnerships

Reames and Kochan (2021) provide a model for effective collaboration focused on relational factors, organizational structures, and operational procedures that support partnership development and sustainability. Based on their model, principals can improve their schools by building trusting relationships with faculty through which they collectively identify local problems and possible solutions, determine how their partnerships can support implementation, and develop ways to sustain change efforts.

This level of trust between principals and faculty is developed over time and reinforced through open communication and district-level support. Organizational structures, including mechanisms for decision-making and obtaining necessary resources, are critical to supporting partnerships. At the school level, principals and faculty establish norms for collaboration that outline their respective roles and responsibilities as well as forms of accountability.

Successful partnerships require resources such as time, personnel, and financial support to operate. Principals and faculty need to ensure there is adequate time for formal and informal activities (e.g., advisory and stakeholder planning meetings), designated personnel, and sufficient financial resources to develop and sustain the partnership. Collaboratively seeking grant funding to support partnerships can further strengthen collaboration. Governmental agencies (e.g., federal and state departments of education) as well as private organizations (e.g., Spencer Foundation) offer grant programs that support research-practice partnerships.

## Developing and Sustaining Partnerships in Schools

There are several considerations for K–12 leaders interested in forming collaborative partnerships with university faculty (see, for example, Haynes et al., 2021; Hudson, 2021; Jimerson et al., 2021). Identifying potential partners within higher education is an important first step for principals. Principals and faculty who understand the local context and share common values can work together to advance the school mission and vision in ways that support teachers and students. Existing partnerships (e.g., for curricular review, program evaluation) can serve as a starting point for further collaboration.

Partnerships should be formed collaboratively with both principals and faculty determining the scope and establishing their respective roles. Sustainability of leadership at the school, district, and university is critical as principals and faculty form and develop partnerships. High turnover among principals, district administration, or faculty disrupts the process of building trusting, long-term relationships among stakeholders.

A planning process that engages motivated stakeholders at the school, district, and university levels is important for determining the scope of the partnership. Developing goals and objectives, activities, and measures of progress should be collaborative. Building trust and fostering open communication help partners establish their respective roles, including expectations and forms of accountability. Periodically revisiting and adjusting roles, as needed, also helps maintain relationships and address partnership goals and objectives.

Engaging in collaborative activities, both formal and informal, is critical to supporting partnerships. Activities related to planning, implementation, and progress monitoring occur at the school as well as the district and university levels. Through strong, trusting relationships, principals and faculty can better share responsibility for decision-making, understand and learn from other's experiences, and increase confidence among stakeholder groups. These reciprocal partnerships help both principals and faculty hone their leadership skills and increase effectiveness in their respective roles.

Collaboratively developing partnership goals and objectives, engaging in formal and informal activities, and determining aligned measures of progress are all necessary for long-term sustainability. For example, research-practice partnerships might be developed to support preservice and induction teachers (e.g., year-long residency programs to increase early career teacher retention), promote high-quality instructional practices (e.g., literacy instruction and assessment strategies to support struggling readers), and provide teacher professional development (e.g., using technology to personalize teacher learning).

By developing clear goals and objectives and planning activities that promote these, principals and faculty are better equipped to determine measures of progress at the school level. Collecting and analyzing data on outcomes helps partners assess whether change aligned with the partnership short- and long-term goals and objectives is happening at the school. Understanding the implications of change, both intended and untended, for students and teachers is particularly important. Through collaboration in these areas, effective partnerships sustained over time offer opportunities for both principals and faculty to develop professionally as leaders.

## SUMMARY

Higher-education institutions offer learning opportunities for K–12 leaders seeking professional growth and career advancement. These include formal opportunities for advanced study through micro-credentials and various graduate-level degree programs as well as informal opportunities for collaborative partnerships between K–12 leaders and university faculty. A practical guide on next steps may be helpful for principals who would like to learn more about available opportunities.

Principals interested in pursuing an advanced degree should begin by exploring available programs and institutions to determine alignment with their own personal and professional goals while also considering the personal and professional implications of returning to graduate school. Professional organizations (e.g., American Educational Research Association, Carnegie Project on the Education Doctorate, University Council for Educational Administration) can be helpful sources of information.

Professional organizations offer a variety of resources for K–12 leaders, including information about professional learning in education generally, specific programs and institutions that may be of interest, and resources that can help support collaborative partnerships. Numerous print and web-based resources (e.g., scholarly and practitioner publications, online forums and blogs, videos) are also available. All of these resources can help K–12 leaders foster learning communities within and beyond higher-education institutions.

## QUESTIONS FOR REFLECTION

The following questions are provided to prompt reflection about opportunities in higher education for K–12 leaders seeking professional learning:

- What are your primary goals for professional growth or career advancement?
- What formal and informal educational experiences would help you reach these goals?
- How would increasing your knowledge base and conducting applied research help you develop as a school leader?

- What personal and professional considerations might influence your decision to pursue an advanced degree? How would you prepare to be successful?
- In what ways can engaging in partnerships with higher-education institutions enhance your efforts to lead change in your school?
- What steps are needed to develop and sustain these partnerships?

## REFERENCES

Browne-Ferrigno, T., & Sanzo, K. L. (2011). Introduction to special issue on university-district partnerships. *Journal of School Leadership, 21*(5), 650–658. https://doi.org/10.1177/105268461102100501

Bryk, A. S., Gomez, L. M., Grunow, A., & LeMahieu, P. G. (2015). *Learning to improve: How America's schools can get better at getting better.* Harvard Education Press.

Dweck, C. S. (2006). *Mindset: The new psychology of success.* Ballantine Books.

Greene, P. (2019, February 16). Education micro-credentials 101: Why do we need badges? *Forbes.* https://www.forbes.com/sites/petergreene/2019/02/16/education-micro-credentials-101-why-do-we-need-badges/?sh=e90d25124190

Haynes, R. L., Sanzo, K. L., & Scribner, J. P. (2021). Factors that contribute to strong district-university partnership: A district stakeholder perspective. In F. Kochan, E. H. Reames, & D. M. Griggs (Eds.), *Partnerships for leadership preparation and development: Facilitators, barriers and models for change* (pp. 77–96). Information Age Publishing Inc.

Hinnant-Crawford, B. N. (2020). *Improvement science in education: A primer.* Myers Education Press.

Hudson, R. L. (2021). Exploring factors that facilitated a K-12 school district/university partnership within a redesigned educational leadership preparation program. In F. Kochan, E. H. Reames, & D. M. Griggs (Eds.), *Partnerships for leadership preparation and development: Facilitators, barriers and models for change* (pp. 37–51). Information Age Publishing Inc.

Hunt, T., Carter, R., Zhang, L., & Yang, S. (2020). Micro-credentials: The potential of personalized professional development. *Development and Learning in Organizations, 34*(2), 33–35. https://doi.org/10.1108/DLO-09-2019-0215

Jimerson, J. B., Atwood, E. D., Cook, K. S., Corder, P. F., & McGhee, M. W. (2021). The principal leadership fellows program: A retrospective look at a partnership-based educational leadership program redesign. In F. Kochan, E. H. Reames, & D. M. Griggs (Eds.), *Partnerships for leadership preparation and development: Facilitators, barriers and models for change* (pp. 37–51). Information Age Publishing Inc.

Kochan, F., Reames, E. H., Serafini, A., & Adair, A. C. (2021). Partnerships in educational leadership preparation and development: What works and what's next? In F. Kochan, E. H. Reames, & D. M. Griggs (Eds.), *Partnerships for leadership preparation and development: Facilitators, barriers and models for change* (pp. 233–243). Information Age Publishing Inc.

Ralston, N. C., Tarasawa, B., Waggoner, J. M., Smith, R., & Naegele, Z. (2016). Developing practitioner-scholars through university-school district research partnerships. *Journal of Public Scholarship in Higher Education, 6*, 94–107.

Reames, E. H., & Kochan, F. (2021). A model for future practice and research. In F. Kochan, E. H. Reames, & D. M. Griggs (Eds.), *Partnerships for leadership preparation and development: Facilitators, barriers and models for change* (pp. 245–259). Information Age Publishing Inc.

Rottman, A. K., & Duggan, M. H. (2021). Micro-credentials in higher education. In J. Keengwe (Ed.), *Handbook of research on innovations in non-traditional educational practices* (pp. 223–236). IGI Global. https://doi.org/10.4018/978-1-7998-4360-3.ch011

U.S. Department of Education, National Center for Education Statistics (NCES). (2019). Table 212.08: Number and percentage distribution of principals in public and private elementary and secondary schools, by selected characteristics: Selected years, 1993–94 through 2017–18. In U.S. Department of Education, National Center for Education Statistics (Ed.), *Digest of education statistics* (2020 ed.). https://nces.ed.gov/programs/digest/d20/tables/dt20_212.08.asp?current=yes

U.S. Department of Education, NCES. (2021). Table 330.50: Average and percentiles of graduate tuition and required fees in degree-granting postsecondary institutions, by control of institution: 1989–90 through 2019–20. In U.S. Department of Education, National Center for Education Statistics (Ed.), *Digest of education statistics* (2020 ed.). https://nces.ed.gov/programs/digest/d20/tables/dt20_330.50.asp?current=yes

Wenger, E., McDermott, R. A., & Snyder, W. (2002). *Cultivating communities of practice: A guide to managing knowledge.* Harvard Business Press.

Westberry, L. A. (2020). *Putting the pieces together: A systems approach to school leadership.* Rowman & Littlefield.

Woods, K. & Woods, J. A. (2021). Less is more: Exploring the value of micro-credentials within a graduate program. *The Journal of Continuing Higher Education.* Advance online publication. https://doi.org/10.1080/07377363.2021.1966923

Young, M. D. (2006). From the director: The M.Ed., Ed.D., and Ph.D. in educational leadership. *UCEA Review, 48*(2), 6–9. http://3fl7112qoj4l3y6ep2tqpwra.wpengine.netdna-cdn.com/wp-content/uploads/2014/07/Summer2006.pdf

*Chapter 7*

# Building a District Leadership Pipeline

Sherry Hoyle and Aaron Allen

## INTRODUCTION

> *A learning organization is an organization that is continually expanding its capacity to create its future.*
>
> —Peter Senge

Essential to the future of a school district's success is the need for a system that serves to develop the leadership capacity of individuals within the organization. Superintendents are currently faced with not only the challenges of impending teacher shortages but also the likelihood of shortages of qualified administrators. Many studies have been conducted that demonstrate the impact that effective administrators have on student and school success (George W. Bush Institute and American Institutes for Research, 2016).

The question becomes what elements are necessary to build sustainable leadership capacity of individuals within the district, whereby creating a system to develop a pool of effective leaders, not just a list of candidates (Day, 2007)? One framework for creating a system for building leadership capacity is the leadership pipeline (Fink, 2011). The leadership pipeline creates a pathway for transitioning the teacher leader, who is aspiring to be an assistant principal, and the assistant principal, who is aspiring to be a principal.

As noted by this pathway, many administrators have begun the journey to the principalship way before actually applying for the job. Developing a leadership pipeline begins with identifying and building capacity in teacher leaders, and providing them with a variety of authentic opportunities to "grow" into leadership roles (Charan & Drotter, 2001). See figure 7.1 below for a model of professional growth.

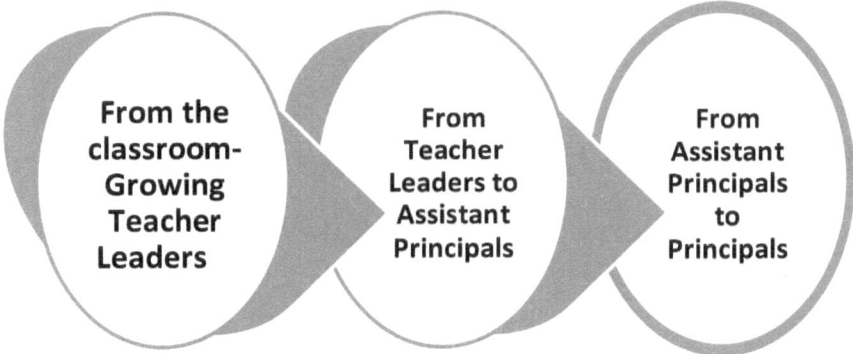

Figure 7.1    Building Leadership Capacity.

## BUILDING LEADERSHIP CAPACITY— GROWING TEACHER LEADERS

When building the leadership capacity of teachers within the school district, the superintendent and district-level staff should work with current administrators to define the profile of what a teacher leader "looks like," develop a plan for nurturing the teachers' leadership capacity, and provide well-defined leadership experiences that encourage teachers to develop leadership skills. When developing a district leadership pipeline one should never underestimate the power of encouraging teachers to explore their leadership capacity.

Goldring and Herrmann (2021) noted that "a study of 15,840 teachers in Miami-Dade County found that teachers who reported being tapped (encouraged by others) were five times more likely to express interest in becoming a principal than teachers who were not tapped (Myung et al., 2011, p. 46)." Leadership pipeline initiatives support the need and importance for districts to create a systemic plan to identify and "grow" teacher leaders into principal candidates (Anderson & Turnbull, 2019).

Leadership pipeline initiatives that purport building leadership capacity within the school district vary from district to district. Each district has the flexibility to choose from a number of options when deciding the best course to pursue based on the district's needs and resources. The first step when identifying and developing professional learning opportunities that nurture teacher leaders is to engage those stakeholders.

These stakeholders provide "real time" input and are currently experiencing the role as an administrator—principals and experienced assistant principals (building-level "experts"), as well as district-level staff who work with administrators or supervise administrators and the superintendent.

Central to the discussion with the key stakeholders involved in the planning process is the determination of what types of "intentional" professional learning opportunities are currently in place in the district, and what additional ones need to be developed. In addition, the conversation with the experts can include, but is not limited to, the following:

- What types of knowledge would be beneficial for aspiring administrators to know?
- What are those skills/knowledge/leadership experiences that you wish you would have known before taking the position? During the first year?
- What experiences contributed to your success as a building-level administrator?
- What opportunities are available at the school and district levels to support the growth of teachers leaders within the district, that is, district grade-level curriculum committees; conduct professional development; lead district-level Professional Learning Communities (PLCs), share and model best practices, coaching, etc.? (This information is obtained from a survey of district-level staff.)

## Building-Level Leadership Opportunities

Westberry (2020), in the book *Putting the Pieces Together: A Systems Approach to School Leadership*, shares a systemic approach for the building-level administrator to utilize in developing teacher leadership capacity at the building level. In her book, she identifies specific activities in which teachers can engage in order to "grow their leadership" skills, that is, "lead professional learning communities; participant in school leadership team meetings; sponsor a student organization, lead a school level Professional Learning Communities (PLC)" (pp. 124–140).

As principals identify and empower teacher leaders at the building level, the next progression is to continue to "grow" those leadership skills by providing ways for the teacher leaders to "stretch" their skills at the district level. Opportunities such as serving on curriculum committees or rural initiatives can provide powerful experiences.

## District-Level Leadership Opportunities

There are a number of ways a district can strategically cultivate teacher leadership capacity by providing tangible opportunities to strengthen, develop, and/or improve leadership skills. For example, as budgets allow, districts create school-level positions that lend themselves for teachers to transition beyond the classroom into positions of leadership, such as content-level facilitators, interventionists, coaches, and so on.

Another strategy incorporated by one school district was to establish a certified position at several of the district's Title I schools that did not have an assistant principal. District-level leadership created a position that was designated as Title I/Assistant Principal. This provided teacher leaders with a venue for exploring the administrative role while still maintaining a direct classroom connection.

Several of the teacher leaders, who were employed in these positions, expressed that the benefits of being a Title I teacher/Assistant Principal afforded them time to explore whether or not they wanted to continue their career trajectory toward administration. They found that the experience did give them confidence in their ability to perform the responsibilities of the role and that it served to give them confidence in their leadership skills. Of those individuals who began in the split position of Title I teacher/Assistant Principal, they went on to acquire full-time assistant principal positions and serve as principals.

Other positions added include the role of an administrative assistant. These individuals serve as quasi administrators in that they are a part of the administrative team but work on a teacher's contract. This position not only saves district funds in administrator allocations but also provides great opportunities for learning with lead teachers.

Additional ways districts implement strategies to develop teacher leadership capacity at the district level include, but are not limited to the following:

1. Co-present with district-level staff at grade level and/or content area meetings, sharing best practices with teachers from across the district.
2. Lead district-level professional development in curriculum and/or instructional practices.
3. Participate on district planning committees, that is, district strategic planning; district-level curriculum committees to develop pacing guides, develop lesson plans, and so on.
4. Apply for positions that are teacher lead positions at the district level, that is, science facilitator, literacy coach, and so on.
5. Serve on district-level advisory committees, that is, district literacy taskforce, and so on.
6. Serve as the school representative on the superintendent's advisory committee.
7. Support teachers presenting at state, regional, and national conferences.
8. Provide teacher leaders with professional learning and networking forums with other teacher leaders across the district through participation in programs, such as a district-level Aspiring Administrators' Academy (AAA).

There are many "moving" parts to developing a systemic plan for building leadership capacity within a district. The time invested "up front" to clearly define the elements of what the district leadership, that is, superintendent, district leadership staff, and selected current principals and assistant principals, envision for developing future administrators from within the district is time well spent.

What are the elements district leadership should consider when building teacher leadership capacity?

1. What is the superintendent, district-level staff, and principal's definition of a "teacher leader"? Along with involving district-level staff, include principals in the process by gathering their feedback. Utilize the collaboration of the different stakeholders, combine and refine the definition to create a picture of "what the teacher leader looks like."
2. What is the vision of a sustainable leadership pipeline that will "grow" leaders from within the district?
3. What are the well-defined leadership opportunities within the district? What types of "intentional" professional learning will be conducted to develop the teachers' leadership skills, that is, "aspiring leadership programs"? Solicit input from current principals regarding what experiences contributed to their success. Survey district-level staff to determine leadership opportunities at the district level, that is, district grade-level curriculum committees; conduct professional development; lead district-level PLCs, share and model best practices, coaching, and so on.
4. What is the plan for communicating the goals, roles, and ways to engage teacher leaders, as previously identified? What training does the superintendent need to facilitate, along with district-level staff, to support building the principal's knowledge of how to identify teacher leaders in his/her school?

As the teacher leaders engage in the well-defined professional learning opportunities at the school and district level, what additional supports can the superintendent and district-level staff put in place in order for the teacher leader to transition to the next level—the assistant principal.

## BUILDING LEADERSHIP CAPACITY—FROM TEACHER LEADER TO ASSISTANT PRINCIPAL

Districts creating leadership pipelines must provide the infrastructure for transitioning the teacher leader into the assistant principal role, and the assistant principal into the principal role. Building core knowledge is one way to support the process of transition. One program that will address the process of building core knowledge is a leadership academy.

By designing an "Aspiring Administrator Academy" (AAA) the superintendent and district staff can create a program that will address learning needs along the leadership continuum. Both teacher leaders who are considering the transition to an assistant principalship, and the assistant principal who would like to transition into a principalship may participate in the AAA. The professional development is structured as a cohort model.

The cohort model allows the same participants who begin the AAA to remain together for the duration of the academy. This is a framework that fosters a supportive and collegial learning environment that results in establishing a professional network that will extend beyond participation in the AAA. The elements of an AAA can be tailored to the district needs, as identified by the superintendent in collaboration with other district staff and principals. What are the elements to consider when designing an AAA?

## Elements to Consider

1. What is the vision for the AAA? What leadership skills and information do the aspiring and current administrators need? The topics of the AAA can be designed to reflect the vision of the superintendent, therefore, the topics may vary. Selected topics may include, but not limited, to "Know Your Path—What Is Your Leadership Style, And Why Does It Matter?"; Leadership and Communication; Equity versus Equality, district processes and procedures; "Systems thinking—What Does It Look Like and Why Do We Need to Think Systemically?"

    *Putting the Pieces Together: A Systems Approach to School Leadership*, by Westberry (2020), is a great resource for future or current administrators. The book provides not only the "why" but also practical examples of what systems thinking looks like when applied in a school setting.

2. Who will be the target audience for the AAA? When considering the transitioning process of leaders to respective levels of the organization, the target group for the AAA can include identified teacher leaders, current assistant principals, and administrative interns. This may differ from the concept of an "induction" program due to the inclusion of stakeholders who are not yet in the assistant principal role, and the depth at which topics are explored.

3. How will the expertise of practitioners, such as principals and district-level staff, be utilized throughout the AAA? Based on the topic designated, principals can serve as "expert speakers" responding to the respective topics and the application "in the field."

4. Will the AAA be the springboard for assistant principals to move into a more focused induction program for assistant principals? Many districts implement assistant principal induction programs. The format of the induction programs is based on the needs of the individual district (Gordon, 2020).

The following agendas (Session 1 and Session 2) reflect a snapshot of one district's AAA. The agendas are examples of two of the three sessions offered in year one of an AAA. The AAA is a two-year professional development for the cohort of teacher leaders and assistant principals from within the district.

## Sample AAA Agenda: Session 1

Aspiring Administrator Academy<br>#Creating a New Path<br>October, February, April<br>Session 1

| | October 26<br>Session 1<br>Know Your Path | |
|---|---|---|
| **Topic/Information** | **Time** | **Agenda** |
| **Welcome** | 1:00 | Presenter: Superintendent<br>• Leadership Profile and Experiences |
| **Leadership 101** | | Presenter: Superintendent<br>Leadership Styles<br>• What type of leader are you?<br>• John Maxwell on Leadership |
| **Leader of Leaders** | | Presenters: Elementary Principal (Current Principal of the Year) and Middle School Principal (Past Principal of the Year)<br>• Lessons Learned from Experience: Lesson 1<br>• Discussion |
| **Leadership Philosophy** | | Presenters: EC Director, Title I Director, MTSS/AIG Director<br>Students First!<br>• Subgroups: All *v.* AIG *v.* EC<br>• EC, 504, ELL<br>• Equity *v.* Equality |
| **Leadership and Communication** | | Presenters: Director of Middle Schools and Director of Technology<br>• Lessons Learned from Experience: Lesson 2 |
| **Homework** | | |

The AAA is a great component of the district leadership pipeline, because it provides teacher leaders a forum for becoming more knowledgeable of what the role of the administrator entails and the district expectations for the role. Strategically, what is the next step for the district plan for those teacher leaders who make the decision to continue their education to seek principal licensure through a preservice preparation program?

## AAA Sample Agenda: Session 2

Aspiring Administrator Academy
#Creating a New Path
October, February, April
Session 2

| | | |
|---|---|---|
| *Session 2* *Follow Your Path* | | |
| **Topic/Information** | **Time** | **Agenda** |
| Welcome | 1:00 | Presenter: Superintendent<br>• Vision<br>• Core Values Exercise |
| Your Life | | Presenters: Elementary Principal and High School Principal<br>• Lessons Learned from Experience: Lesson 3<br>• Discussion |
| Managing Time | | Presenters: Director of Elementary, Director of Middle Schools, and Director of High Schools<br>Instructional Time<br>• Scheduling Workshop<br>• Vertical Alignment and Transitions<br>• PD Initiatives |
| Avoid Derailment | | Presenter: Assistant Superintendent of Curriculum and Instruction<br>• What causes educational leaders to derail? |
| Apply to be a Principal | | Director of Human Resources<br>• Application Process for the Administrator |
| New Principal Focus Group | | Presenters: New Principals<br>• Must know do's and don'ts for a new principal |

## District-Level Supported Leadership Opportunities

Preservice preparation programs for a district leadership pipeline can be unique in that it does not take the traditional program route. The university-district partnerships ensure that the university and the school district align efforts and expectations. What does this look like? One such program is the *Leaders for Tomorrow* or Project *LfT*. The *LfT* is a partnership between Winthrop University's (located in Rock Hill, South Carolina) Educational Leadership Program and Charlotte Mecklenburg Schools (CMS).

The partnership is multifaceted from the selection of candidates to the collaboration in customizing the curriculum for the program. In regard to selection of candidates, CMS has developed a system for building-level principals to nominate teacher candidates from within the school buildings. CMS has clearly defined the "vision" of what the teacher leader should "look like" if selected for the *LfT*. The nominated candidates then complete an application to the graduate school at Winthrop University and must successfully complete a screening process by the Winthrop University Educational Leadership faculty.

Components of the screening process are modeled after the CMS assistant principal screening protocol used by the human resources department in CMS. This simulation gives candidates experience with what to expect when they complete the program and apply for an assistant principal position in the CMS district.

In addition, Winthrop University partners with CMS to collaboratively design a two-year master's in educational leadership program that addresses national and North Carolina State standards and requirements, while customizing the curriculum to address key issues, topics, and practices in the CMS system. The content is then delivered by Winthrop University faculty who utilize CMS staff as guest speakers, adjunct instructors, or guest lecturers.

Embedding the use of the CMS staff within the course delivery exposes candidates to various staff within the district, as well as specific content that is germane to CMS schools. It also provides a networking opportunity for the candidates, and allows the CMS staff to become familiar with the candidates. The advantage for the district is having a strong pool of applicants who are familiar with district initiatives, practices, and who have had the opportunity to engage with district staff. College and school district partnerships, in which curriculum is aligned to employer expectations, are the strongest (Yendel-Hoppey et al., 2017).

Another example of districts partnering with universities is the High Point University's Leadership Academy (HPULA). Developing future administrators not is only a priority within school districts but also has the attention of legislators in North Carolina. As a result of a competitive grant sponsored by the North Carolina General Assembly, High Point University (HPU), located in High Point, North Carolina, was awarded five years of funding in the amount of $4,400,000. The grant was secured in order to support aspiring administrators as they pursed a master's in educational leadership and also during the internship period of their program.

The design of the program is focused on preparing leaders to help bring transformation to school environments of high-risk and under-performing schools. HPU partners with fourteen school districts to offer a leadership academy. As a result of the grant the HPULA Program is able to fully fund the tuition of each candidate, as well as, provide a salary for the internship experience.

During the internship year when the candidate performs a full-time internship, he/she is assigned by the home district to a location of the district's choosing. This allows the district staff to work with the administrative intern to determine the best school placement based on the needs of the district, as well as the area of growth needed for the intern. For example, one district placed an intern, whose teaching career was at the middle level, at the elementary level in order to broaden his experience level. This flexibility allows the district to monitor the strengths of the candidate and skill set to consider for future administrative placement.

The effectiveness of the principal pipelines and the district-university partnerships have received favorable reviews based on a report by the Rand Corporation Report (Gates et al., 2019), *Principal Pipelines: A Feasible, Affordable, Effective Way for Districts to Improve Schools*, funded by the Wallace Foundation. Jody Spiro, the director of education leadership at the foundation, said in an interview, "These pipelines are systemic, strategic, district-wide strategies to change systems in order to use leadership as a lever for improving student achievement, particularly in the lowest-performing schools" (Jacobson, 2019, p. 2).

As individuals continue progressing through the district's leadership pipeline what professional learning opportunities are available for assistant principals if they are interested in progressing to the next administrative level—the principalship? When planning and developing the district leadership pipeline, what systems need to be in place to "grow" assistant principals into principals?

Many districts take a multipronged approach by doing the following: (1) create an Assistant Principals Induction Program (APIP), (2) assign an experienced assistant principal mentor, and (3) provide support for the assistant principal that would empower him/her to take an active role in initiating conversations with his/her principal mentor. Those conversations would involve the assistant principal conveying his/her desire to have the opportunity to assume more leadership roles, be challenged, and move out of his/her comfort zone, as defined by the individual and principal mentor.

## BUILDING LEADERSHIP CAPACITY—FROM ASSISTANT PRINCIPALS TO PRINCIPALS

### Principal Mentor

Hutton (2020) raises the question regarding whether or not assistant principals are prepared to become principals.

> The readiness of assistant principals is dependent largely on two things: (1) the types and structure of experiences their principals provide within the context of the school day, and (2) their principals' attitudes toward outside leadership opportunities. Principals must share power, employing shared decision-making models to build the leadership capacity of all their colleagues and staff, giving their assistant principals autonomy to allow them to identify and build leadership skills. The readiness and success of assistant principals can be predicted by the nature and extent of the instructional leadership experiences they have. (p. 42)

It has been noted the most effective professional learning occurs when the opportunity to learn is job-embedded, real-time situations where the assistant principal can take the leadership role, but also have the "safety net" of the principal mentor's close availability, if needed. The superintendent and district-level staff must ensure that assistant principals have a principal mentor who possesses the capacity to answer the superintendent's question, *"How are you developing the assistant principal into a leader versus just a manager?"*

If the superintendent's expectation is that the principal provides opportunities that will challenge and grow the assistant principal, allowing him/her to assume more leadership roles, be challenged, and move out of his/her comfort zone—what does that look like in action during day-to-day operations?

Does the principal mentor allow the assistant principal to lead, plan, and coordinate events? Does the principal allow the assistant principal to take the lead when conducting walkthroughs or observations, and then follow up with meaningful conversations about what was observed? Does the principal mentor provide opportunities for the assistant principal to attend meetings with civic leaders and other community organizations? Does the assistant principal take an active role in initiating conversations with his/her principal mentor regarding areas for growth?

The most effective and efficient administrative school teams have been those where the principal mentor has shared the leadership roles and responsibilities, allowing and empowering the assistant principal to stretch his/her leadership skills in an environment of trust and support—an environment where mistakes are viewed as failing forward and regarded as opportunities for learning and continuous improvement. In addition to a principal mentor, district leadership pipeline plans have also incorporated more intense, job-specific professional learning by offering Assistant Principal Induction Programs (APIPs).

## Assistant Principal Induction Program

Hutton (2020) maintains that "assistant principals typically do not receive any professional development in the areas to which they are traditionally assigned—student conflict, staff relations, and facilities management" (pp. 41–42). The APIP is a more focused training approach than the AAA addressed earlier in the chapter. The principal induction program becomes a forum for strategically and intentionally providing professional learning sessions addressing topics specifically applicable to the challenges, roles, and responsibilities of the assistant principal.

This type of program delves deeper into the leadership role while also leveraging the time to explore the principalship. The design and format of the APIP is based on the needs of the individual district (Gordon, 2020). The length of the induction sessions and the topics will vary. School districts design APIP around topics that are pertinent to school leadership and the operation protocols of the individual district.

Examples of APIP topics can include, but are not limited to, the following:

1. How to Have Crucial Conversations
2. Almost Everything I Need to Know About Operations and Facilities (There Will Always Be Surprises!)
3. How to Develop a Positive Culture in a Challenging Environment
4. The Nuts and Bolts of Budgets and School Finance
5. How to Create and Maintain a Common Vision and Mission
6. How to Lead for Continuous Improvement

District "experts" are utilized as presenters for each topic. The structure of the sessions will revolve around a guest presenter, group discussion, case studies based on the session topic, application to the assistant principals' schools, and when applicable, homework is given. Studies consistently report that assistant principals' formal and informal mentoring and networking are important for their development.

## Principal Leadership Opportunities for the Assistant Principal

Other avenues that districts have provided learning opportunities for assistant principals include job assignments from the district office that allow the assistant principal to fulfill the roles and responsibilities of the principal for an interim period of time. For example, one district employs assistant principals to serve as summer school principals. The district leadership views this as a chance for the assistant principal to authentically experience the role of principal.

The summer school principal is in charge of all aspects of leading a school and all the decision-making that is involved during the course of the summer school session(s). This is a great setting for putting demands on leadership skills to quickly establish a culture of learning when bringing together teachers from across the district. Assistant principals selected as the summer school principals have been given opportunities to grow and experience problem-solving on demand, as is the case so often in the principalship.

The same district also provides leadership options for assistant principals to serve as principal substitutes throughout the school year. The district's alternative school and several elementary schools do not have assistant principal positions due to low enrollment. Therefore, the district assigns assistant principals the role of being the "principal for a day," assigned to a school where the principal may be absent due to either illness, professional development, or absent due to family issues.

Not only does this approach assist with coverage at the school, it also exposes assistant principals to different grade spans other than the one in which they work, especially when serving as administrative coverage for the alternative school. Assistant principals must learn to quickly adjust and provide support as needed. They become the final support for a day, and this can be illuminating in many ways.

Goldring et al.'s (2021) analysis of "multiple studies found that assistant principals valued professional interactions, whether through professional networks, on-the-job mentoring, or learning by doing" (p. 53). In addition, to the authentic experiences as the lead principal, the APIP, and effective principal mentoring, what are other elements should the district leadership identify for this level of the leadership pipeline?

## District Considerations

1. What opportunities do the superintendent and district-level leadership make available for personalized leadership development? Just as teachers provide personalized learning opportunities for students, so should the superintendent consider what types of personalized leadership

development is needed for each assistant principal based on his/her strengths and areas for improvement?
2. What are the well-defined leadership opportunities for assistant principals within the district? During the summer months many districts conduct summer school for remediation and/or enrichment for students. By allowing assistant principals the opportunity to assume the "principal role" for the summer sessions, he/she has the opportunity to really experience the role of the principal on a smaller scale.
3. What professional development opportunities are available for the assistant principal who aspires to move into the principal role? What types of intentional professional learning will be conducted to develop the assistant principals' leadership. One forum for professional development is the implementation of PLCs.

Are ongoing leadership PLCs available? The leadership PLCs for assistant principals should involve authentic and/or "just in time" training for topics that are applicable to the principalship. The PLC provides a forum for networking and focused professional development that is germane to the needs of the assistant principal who will be transitioning to the role of principal.

As districts continue to build leadership capacity from within, superintendents should consider how to leverage external resources. Partnerships with universities and businesses can serve to garner many avenues of support in developing and sustaining the leadership pipeline.

## Building Leadership Capacity through Partnerships—Higher Education and Business

As noted earlier in the chapter, district-university partnerships can play a vital role in a district's plan to develop leadership capacity within the district. No longer relying on formal preparation programs alone, districts have taken the initiative to partner with universities in order to influence programmatic elements that serve to inform university programs (MacFarlane et al., 2015).

Working together, districts and universities meet to discuss how district priorities, curricular initiatives, and practices can be integrated throughout the coursework in the university's educational leadership program. In addition, the university utilizes district leaders to serve as guest speakers, thought partners, and/or serve on the university's program advisory committee.

Districts and universities have also partnered with corporations to collaboratively develop a curriculum rich in leadership experiences that span effective leadership practice not only in an educational setting but also in the business field. This serves to provide a broader perspective of leadership utilizing the different lenses from various career fields. One example of districts, universities, and businesses collaborating to work with aspiring leaders is HPU in High Point, North Carolina.

HPU has formed the High Point University Leadership Academy. This leadership academy is committed to providing a rigorous, research-based curriculum, developed by working collaboratively with district personnel and affiliates such as the Center for Creative Leadership, the BB&T Leadership Institute, and the National Conference for Community & Justice.

The School Executive Leadership Academy (SELA) partners Queens McColl School of Business, Queens Cato School of Education, and local CMS as a way to provide an accelerated option for developing building-level leaders. The program has the combined expertise of the School of Business faculty in developing leaders, along with the School of Education's and the school districts' expertise in education. The program engenders an experiential approach centered on simulations and a variety of scenarios that reflects the challenges of the administrator.

As district leadership is faced with ensuring that there is a pool of highly qualified administrators, growing leaders at all levels of the organization require a systemic approach that maximizes a network of support and collaboration with school districts, higher education, and business. Developing and sustaining a robust leadership pipeline of competent and caring administrators is everyone's responsibility.

## SUMMARY

Building a district leadership pipeline that nurtures leadership capacity at all levels of the organization (see figure 7.2 below) has become more critical as districts are faced with the challenges of hiring highly skilled administrators who can seamlessly transition into a leadership role. Districts have the flexibility based on the need and resources available to design a plan to build leadership capacity from the teacher level to the principal level.

However, vital to the district plan is the need to create a systemic, sustainable approach to building leadership capacity from within the district that will reap benefits long-term. The plan should include professional learning opportunities for teacher leaders to "grow" and expand their leadership skill set beyond the classroom and building level to the district level. Similarly, assistant principals should be given opportunities to assume roles and responsibilities of shared leadership with the principal in order to develop, improve, or polish those skills necessary for moving to the next role—the principalship.

Professional learning opportunities for teacher leaders and assistant principals can take on many forms. Some of which include, but are not limited

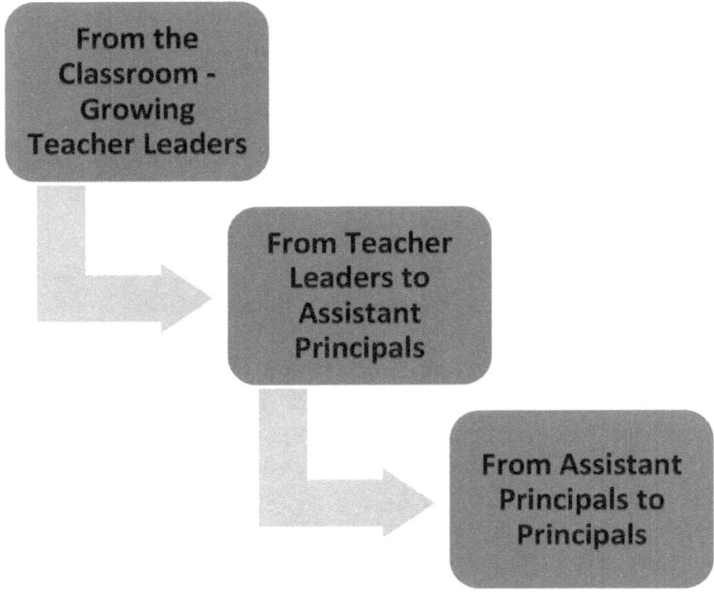

Figure 7.2 Building a Leadership Pipeline from within the District.

to the following: AAA; partnerships with universities to custom design leadership programs to meet the needs of the district within the parameters of national and state leadership standards; partnerships with business/industry to share leadership expertise; APIPs; and principal mentors.

## QUESTIONS FOR REFLECTION

- What is the district's definition of a teacher leader?
- How can the district demonstrate support for leaders at all levels of the organization?
- How does the district benefit from a district leadership pipeline that nurtures individuals' leadership capacity from within the district?
- What elements must be included in a systemic approach to developing a district leadership pipeline?
- What approach should the superintendent have when developing leaders at each level of the organization and why?

## REFERENCES

Anderson, L. M., & Turnbull, B. J. (2019). *Sustaining a principal pipeline. Policy Studies Associates and the Wallace Foundation, 18,* 18, 43. https://www

.wallacefoundation.org/knowledge-center/Documents/Sustaining-a-Principal-Pipeline.pdf

Charan, R., Drotter, S., & Noel, J. (2001). *The leadership pipeline.* Jossey-Bass.

Day, D. (2007). *Developing leadership talent: A guide to succession planning and leadership development.* Human Resource Management Foundation. https://www.shrm.org/hr-today/trends-and-forecasting/special-reports-and-expert-views/Documents/Developing-Leadership-Talent.pdf

Fink, D. (2011). Pipelines, pools and reservoirs: Building leadership capacity for sustained improvement. *Journal of Educational Administration, 49*(6), 670–684.

Gates, S. M., Baird, M. D., Master, B. K., & Chavez-Herrerias, E. R. (2019). *Principal pipelines: A feasible, affordable, effective way for districts to improve schools.* Rand Corporation.

George W. Bush Institute and American Institutes for Research. (2016). *Principal talent management according to the evidence: A review of the literature,* 5. http://gwbcenter.imgix.net/Resources/gwbi-principal-talent-management-lit-review.pdf

Goldring, E., Rubin, M., & Herrmann, M. (2021). *The role of assistant principals: Evidence and insights for advancing school leadership.* The Wallace Foundation. https://www.wallacefoundation.org/knowledge-center/pages/the-role-of-assistant-principals-evidence-insights-for-advancing-school-leadership.aspx

Gordon, S. (2020). The principal development pipeline: A call for collaboration. *NASSP Bulletin, 104*(2), 61–84. https://doi.org/10.1177/0192636520923404

Hutton, B. (2020, April). Shared leadership: Reculturing the assistant principal ship. *Principal Leadership, 20*(8), 41–45.

Jacobson, L. (2019, April 8). *Principal pipeline districts see stronger student achievement gains, retention.* K-12 Dive. https://www.k12dive.com/news/principal-pipeline-districts-see-stronger-student-achievement-gains-retent/551977/

MacFarlane, J. R., Riley, D. L., & Turnbul, B. J. (2015). Districts taking charge of the principal pipeline. *Policy Studies Associates, Inc, 3,* 41–61.

Myung, J., Loeb, S., & Horng, E. (2011). Tapping the principal pipeline: Identifying talent for future school leadership in the absence of formal succession management programs. *Educational Administration Quarterly, 47*(5), 695–727. https://doi.org/10.1177/0013161X11406112

Turnbull, B. J., Anderson, L. M., Riley, D. L., MacFarlane, J. R., & Aladjem, D. K. (2016). *Building a stronger principalship, vol. 5: The principal pipeline initiative in action.* Policy Studies Associates, Inc., and RAND Corporation. https://www.wallacefoundation.org/knowledge-center/pages/building-a-stronger-principalship-vol-5-the-principal-pipeline-initiative-in-action.aspx

Westberry, L. (2020). *Putting the pieces together: A systems approach to school leadership.* Rowman & Littlefield.

Yendol-Hoppey, D., Shanely, D., Delane, D. C., & Hoppey, D. T. (Eds.). (2017). *Working together: Enhancing urban educator quality through school-university partnerships.* Information Age Publishing, Inc.

# About the Authors

### PREFACE

**Lee A. Westberry** is an assistant professor of educational leadership in the Zucker Family School of Education at The Citadel Military College in Charleston, South Carolina. She also serves as the program coordinator for the Division of Ed Leadership and the director of program development and enhancement for the ZFSOE. She provides principal professional development across the state and has recently published new books entitled *Putting the Pieces Together: A Systems Approach to School Leadership*, *The Final Piece: A Systems Approach to School Leadership*, and *The Virtual Principal: The Many Facets of the Demanding Job*. Her primary research interests include principal leadership, systems, and professional development.

### CHAPTER 1

**Sally Zepeda** is a professor of educational administration and policy at the University of Georgia in the Mary Frances Early College of Education. Her research examines the intersections between job-embedded professional learning, supervision, and evaluation and the development of teachers and building- and district-level leaders.

**Salih Cevik** is a PhD candidate in the Educational Administration and Policy Program at the University of Georgia. He obtained his master's degree in educational leadership and policy at the University of Minnesota. His research focuses on differentiated instruction, teacher evaluation, and social justice.

**Sevda Yildirim** is a PhD candidate in the Educational Administration and Policy Program at the University of Georgia. Her research interests are teacher evaluation and supervision practices and policies, and the implementation of professional development. Prior to coming to the University of Georgia, she earned a MEd in educational leadership at the University of Florida.

## CHAPTER 2

**R. Stewart Mayers** is a professor in and chair of the Department of Educational Instruction and Leadership and director of teacher education at Southeastern Oklahoma State University. His research interests include trust in leadership and legal issues in employee and student social-media usage.

**Jennifer Anderson** is an assistant professor of educational instruction and leadership at Southeastern Oklahoma State University. Her research interests include school and district leadership, the use of data to inform decisions and drive change, education equity and opportunity, and the impacts of state and federal education policy.

## CHAPTER 3

**Arvin D. Johnson** is an associate professor of educational leadership at Kennesaw State University. He has been in the field of education for more than twenty-two years. His research interests are principal professional learning and preparation, pedagogy and curriculum, and school finance.

## CHAPTER 4

**Sherry Hoyle** currently serves as an assistant professor in the Department of Educational Leadership at Winthrop University, Rock Hill, South Carolina. She has been on faculty since 2017. Prior to her tenure at Winthrop University she has served in many district-level leadership roles ranging from superintendent, assistant superintendent, director of elementary education to the building level during her thirty-eight years in education. She received her doctorate in Educational Leadership from the University of North Carolina at Charlotte.

## CHAPTER 5

**Kevin Badgett** is an associate professor and department chair for Educational Leadership in the College of Education at the University of Texas Permian Basin. In addition to his experience at UTPB, he has served in various roles in the K–12 setting as a teacher, school counselor, and campus and district-level administrator. His research interests include school-community relations, leadership effectiveness, and teacher retention.

**Larry G. Daniel** is dean and professor in the College of Education at The University of Texas Permian Basin. His forty-plus-year career in education includes service as a middle/high school educator, an education professor, and a higher-education leader. His areas of scholarly interest include educational leadership, teacher education, educational policy, and quantitative research methods.

## CHAPTER 6

**Noelle Paufler** is an assistant professor of educational leadership and coordinator for the Doctor of Education (EdD) in Education Systems Improvement Science Program at Clemson University. She has experience as a high school social studies teacher, district administrator, and applied researcher in high-need districts and schools.

## CHAPTER 7

**Sherry Hoyle** currently serves as an assistant professor in the Department of Educational Leadership at Winthrop University, Rock Hill, South Carolina. She has been on faculty since 2017. Prior to her tenure at Winthrop University she has served in many district-level leadership roles ranging from superintendent, assistant superintendent, director of elementary education to the building level during her thirty-eight years in education. She received her doctorate in Educational Leadership from the University of North Carolina at Charlotte.

**Aaron Allen** is an adjunct instructor at the University of North Carolina Charlotte in the Educational Leadership Department, as well as the superintendent of Lincoln County Schools (NC). Of his twenty-three years in education, he has also served as associate superintendent, assistant superintendent, director of human resources, principal, assistant principal, high school teacher, coach, county athletic director, and athletic trainer. He is an advocate for public education and considers himself a coach of students, adults, and community members striving to make his community and region the best place to be.

www.ingramcontent.com/pod-product-compliance
Lightning Source LLC
Chambersburg PA
CBHW030144240426
43672CB00005B/257